free for
the eating

OTHER BOOKS BY THE AUTHOR

HOME IN YOUR PACK

MISTER RIFLEMAN
  (with Colonel Townsend Whelen)

WE LIKE IT WILD

WILDERNESS COOKERY

HOW TO GO LIVE IN THE WOODS ON $10 A WEEK

ON YOUR OWN IN THE WILDERNESS
  (with Colonel Townsend Whelen)

LIVING OFF THE COUNTRY

HOW TO BUILD YOUR HOME IN THE WOODS

AT HOME IN THE WOODS

bradford angier

free for

the eating

STACKPOLE BOOKS
Harrisburg, Pennsylvania

For Jack Otis

and for Gundy

Contents

Consult the Directory of Wild Plants on page 8 to locate
instantly all wild plants treated in this book.

Directory

# of Wild Plants

ACKNOWLEDGMENTS

The author is indebted for some of the illustrations to: New York State College of Agriculture at Cornell University and their bulletin, *Wild Foods,* by Eva L. Gordon, the U.S. Department of Agriculture, and Vena Angier.

Free for the Eating

The pick of the wild foods will upgrade your meals when you're camping, fishing, and hunting. But that's a very minor part of their value! Back home, no matter where you live, they'll keep right on guaranteeing you some of the best eating there is—plus the continued incentive to get outdoors where the really healthy appetites are born.

Wild foods have always been important in this young country. The Pilgrims derived considerable nourishment during their first desperate winter from groundnuts, which are

11

similar to small potatoes. California's Forty-Niners, plagued by scurvy because of the scarcity of fresh food in some of the gold camps, were introduced to miner's lettuce by the Indians and Spanish. Farther north, scurvy grass performed a similar function, both preventing and curing the vitamin-deficiency disease among early frontiersmen. When regular rations on the Lewis and Clark expedition had to be reduced to one biscuit a day, it was the sweet yellow fruit of the papaw that kept the men going.

In almost any rural or suburban neighborhood you will find within a few minutes of home far more wild edibles than you can eat. There is no need to venture into the deep woods. In fact, you'll find more wild foods around vacant buildings, deserted farms, old pastures, fields, walls and fences, open hillsides, the edges of woodlands, marshes, streams, lakes and ponds, burned-over sections, along roads, and in your own yard. In large and small cities, vacant lots will yield a surprising harvest.

With countless pesticides gradually poisoning the cultivated areas of North America, it's both healthful and pleasant to go into the open places and gather undefiled foods from Nature's own pure garden. Too, these wild delicacies have been uncontaminated by the dozens of human hands that handle and rehandle the fruits and vegetables sold by markets.

As for possible poisoning, it is just as easy to become poisoned by eating the leaves of garden rhubarb or the sprouts or greened skins of ordinary potatoes. There are thousands of edible wild plants in North America and only a limited number of poisonous plants. In the Arctic, for example, all properly prepared plants are edible with the exception of one mushroom.

You don't need to be any sort of an expert to begin taking advantage of this free food. If you will surely identify everything before you pick it—and this book, with its detailed descriptions and drawings, not only affords ample means for doing this, but also eliminates borderline plants that might reasonably cause confusion—you will never have any trouble. Start with just a few wild edibles, if you want, perhaps with those you've already known for years, although perhaps not as foods. Each year add a few more.

There is one more consideration which, as world conditions continue to worsen almost by the day, is becoming increasingly important. Anyone at any time can suddenly find himself dependent on his own resources for enough food to keep himself and his family alive. It costs very little time and effort to be ready for such an emergency. If you are not ready, it may cost your life.

You may become lost or stranded in the wilderness. Thousands among North America's millions of campers, fishermen, and hunters do each year, many fatally. Yet almost invariably, where such individuals suffer and all too needlessly die, a choice of wild foods is free for the eating.

You may be in a vehicle that is stalled by mishap or storm in an unsettled area, a not too uncommon occurrence that frequently results in unnecessary hardship, if not worse. Perhaps you'll be in an aircraft that crashes or has to make a forced landing. Perhaps you'll be shipwrecked or isolated by flood.

It may even happen that you and yours will be compelled to seek sanctuary in the outdoors because of those ever increasing threats to civilization itself—an atom bomb catastrophe or the even more terrible microscopic foes of germ warfare.

Adding from season to season the recognition of a few more edible wild plants can be an engrossing and practical hobby, as well as a thrifty and healthful way of pleasantly introducing new delicacies to your table. Such acquired knowledge can even mean, in some unforeseen emergency, the difference between eating bountifully and starving.

And they're all free for the eating.

Wild Fruits

It's difficult to travel across a corner of North America, from the very deserts to the glittering ice cakes of the Arctic Ocean, that doesn't regularly yield wholesome and often delectable wild fruit.

Besides the numerous common grapes, cherries, and plums, the uniquely flavored little wintergreens, and the crab apples, that thrive wild from the southern states to Alaska, there are the startlingly red but less familiar berries of the staghorn sumac that, crushed in water and sweetened, give a drink like lemonade. Also not to be overlooked are the sustaining red berries of the kinnikinic, whose leaves are still a familiar backwoods tobacco substitute.

It's not hard to find the common blueberries, gooseberries, cranberries, and their ilk that every year fill out by the thousands of tons. And there are such abounding members of the rose family as strawberries, blackberries, and raspberries, whose young stems and stalks are also tasty, and whose leaves can be profitably steeped for tea.

PRICKLY PEAR *(Opuntia)*

There is also the unlikely prickly pear—the little thorny knobs, ranging from the size of apricots to the size of large lemons, that bulge from the padlike joints of cactus. Actually, the spine-bristling skin of this fruit of the cactus is so unmistakable that any difficulties lie not in identifying but in picking. It's best to go about this with leather gloves and a knife.

Depending on the kind of cactus, the ripened colors of prickly pears vary from tawny green and purplish black to the choicest of them all—the big red fruits of the large *Opuntia megacantha* of the continental Southwest. To eat any of these Indian figs, as they're also known, slice off the ends, slit the hide lengthways, and scoop out the pulp.

ROSE *(Rosa)*

Delicious wild foods grow everywhere. For example, there is a familiar berry that, although you've maybe never sampled it, has the flavor of fresh apples. More important, its juice is from six to twenty-four times richer in Vitamin C than even orange juice. Throughout much of the continent you can pick all you want the greater part of the year, even when temperatures fall a booming 60° below zero. As for recognizing the fruit, no one with a respect for brambles and a modicum of outdoor knowledge is going to get the wrong thing by mistake. It is the rose hip, the ordinary seed pod of roses everywhere.

Some thirty-five or more varieties of wild roses thrive throughout the United States, especially along streams, roadsides, fences, open woods, and in meadows, often forming briary thickets. The hips or haws, somewhat roundly smooth and contracted to a neck on top, grow from characteristically fragrant flowers, usually pink, white, or red. Remaining on the shrubs throughout the winter and into the following spring, they are available for food in the North when other sources of nourishment are covered with snow.

ROSE
Hips, Leaves, and Stems.

These rose hips have a delicate flavor that's delectable. They're free. They're strong medicine, to boot. Studies in Idaho found the scurvy-preventing vitamin in the raw pulp running from 4,000 to nearly 7,000 milligrams a pound. Daily human requirements, estimated to be 60 to 75 milligrams, provide a yardstick for this astonishing abundance.

Three rose hips, the food experts say, have as much Vitamin C as an orange. We don't pay much attention to these gratuitous vitamins in the United States and Canada. But in England during World War II, some five million pounds of rose hips were gathered from the roadsides and put up to take the place of then scarce citrus fruits. Dried and powdered, rose hips are sold in Scandinavian countries for use in soups, for mixing with milk or water to make hot and cold drinks, for sprinkling over cereals, etc., all of which they do admirably.

This cousin of the apple, one of the many members of the rose family, is nutritious whether eaten off the bushes, cut up in salad, baked in cake or bread, or boiled into jam or jelly. As a matter of fact, plain dried rose hips are well worth carrying in a pocket for lunching on like raisins. To prepare them for this latter use, just cut each in half. Remove the central core of seeds. Dry the remaining shell-like skin and pulp quickly in a cool oven or in a kettle suspended above the fringes of a small campfire.

One good way to use rose hips is turn them into syrup. Snip the bud ends from a freshly gathered batch. Then cover the fruit with water and boil rapidly until soft. Strain off the juice. Return the pulp to the kettle, add enough water to cover, and make a second extraction. For every 2 cups juice, add 1 cup sugar. Boil until thick. Pour into sterilized bottles. That's all. Poured over steaming sourdough pancakes on blue-black mornings when the Northern Lights are still ablaze, this syrup never lasts long.

Here's an extra hint. Don't throw away the pulp. Press it through a sieve to remove seeds and skins. Add one half as much sugar as pulp. Put in clove, cinnamon, and any other spices or flavoring agents to taste. Heat covered until the sugar is dissolved. Then uncover and cook slowly until thick, stirring to prevent sticking. Pack in sterilized jars and seal. Voila! Fruit butter.

With rose hips up to sixty times richer in Vitamin C than lemon juice—and richer in iron, calcium, and phosphorus than oranges—you might as well get the most good out of them while insuring maximum flavor. The best way to do this is to use the rose hips the day they are picked and to gather them while they are red but slightly underripe on a dry, sunny day.

But even after frost or later in the winter when they are shriveled and dry, rose hips are still worth picking. Earlier in the season, the petals themselves, varying in flavor like different species of apples, are delicious if you discard the bitterish green or white bases. Dark red roses are strong-tasting, the flavors becoming more delicate as colors become subdued through the light pinks.

Even the seeds are valuable, being rich in Vitamin E. Some backwoods wives grind them, boil in a small amount of water, and then strain through a cloth. The resulting vitamin-rich fluid is used in place of the water called for in recipes for syrups, jams, and jellies.

The flowers make a rather tasty tea, if each heaping tea-spoon of dried petals, twice that amount of fresh petals, is covered with a cup of boiling water, then steeped for five minutes. A little honey or sugar helps bring out the fragrance. Leaves, roots, and the rose hips themselves are also occasionally used for tea.

BLUEBERRY *(Vaccinium)* *(Gaylussacia)*

Like numerous other members of the heath family, the blueberry genus thrives in acid soil, and I've seen thousands of acres of new bushes, heavy with berries, spreading over fire-blackened lands in Maine. Although botanists differ, some thirty-five different members of this species, from low shrubs to high bushes, grow throughout the United States and Canada, mostly in open woods and clearings. None is poisonous. Other names include whortleberries and bilberries.

One major difference among the many varieties is between so-called blueberries and huckleberries which, if you care, is easily resolved. Blueberries proper have many fine, easily chewable seeds. Huckleberries, which also have distinguishing waxy spots on their foliage and fresh shoots, contain ten larger seeds. Blueberries and huckleberries are good eating throughout the continent. A few species, though, it should be added, take on their true goodness only after being cooked, as you can readily find out for yourself.

BLUEBERRY
Left: in flower; *Right:* with fruit.

A lot of game is the tastier for these mostly sweet, juicy, generally reddish to blue and blackish-purple berries, which, too, sometimes ripen to a greenish or yellowish color. Black bear roasts and stews are especially choice when these animals have been putting on fat by stuffing themselves with blueberries. Several species of grouse feed mainly on blueberries summers and early falls. Deer, moose, and rabbits browse on the foliage, fruit, and pretty little bell-shaped flowers.

Blueberries commonly grow so thick that you can often gather them by the bushel, stripping them indiscriminately in large handfuls or shaking them onto spread sheets. One way to clean them later is to drop them, a few at a time, from the pails onto a slanted blanket, tightly stretched a few feet below. Let the ripe blueberries roll into a large wide basin set just below the lower edge of the blanket. Most of the harder green berries will bounce free. The leaves and twigs will remain on the blanket, which can occasionally be brushed clean. Finally, rolled around in water to remove a little more debris, the plunder will be ready to eat.

This fruit excels in pies. Here's the best way we know of going about a blueberry pie. This pie isn't so solid with thickeners such as arrowroot, tapioca, or cornstarch that it will hold solidly together while you punctuate the occasional forkful with conversation. As a matter of fact, most diners who sit down to this particular dessert find they are glad to hold up on the repartee awhile and to finish off with a spoon.

All you need besides the pastry is 4 cups fresh blueberries, 1 cup sugar, and ¼ cup melted butter or margarine. As for the cooking, it takes place in a single operation. Line a greased pie pan with pastry. Mix the berries, sugar, and shortening. Pour them into the uncooked shell. Top with the upper crust, being sure to cut vents. Bake in a preheated oven, moderately hot, about 50 minutes, or until the crust is golden tan.

Or maybe on occasion you'd prefer blueberry slump. For this, bring 4 cups blueberries, 1½ cups sugar, 4 tablespoons cornstarch, and 1 teaspoon nutmeg slowly to a boil in a heavy saucepan.

While the mixture is heating, make a batter by first creaming 4 tablespoons of sugar with 3 tablespoons of shortening.

Add ⅓ cup milk and blend thoroughly. Mix 1½ cups sifted flour, 1½ teaspoons baking powder, and ¼ teaspoon salt. Stir rapidly into the other ingredients.

Then begin dropping the batter, spoonful by spoonful, over the bubbling berries. Cover and cook at the same speed for 10 minutes. Serve hot with cream, milk, or vanilla ice cream.

Hot blueberry frying-pan bread, good anywhere, is especially easy to cook when you're away on vacation. The following basic mix, given here in man-and-wife proportions, will stay fresh for 6 weeks or more in camp if kept sealed, dry, and reasonably cool. For it you'll need: 2 cups all-purpose flour, 3 teaspoons double action baking powder, ½ teaspoon salt, and 6 tablespoons oleomargarine.

If this mix is being readied at home, sift the flour before measuring it. Then sift together the flour, baking powder, and salt. Cut in the margarine with 2 knives, with an electric mixer at low speed, or with a pastry blender until the mixture resembles coarse meal. For somewhat better flavored and more nourishing bread, add 4 tablespoons of powdered skim milk.

Place in plastic bags. Seal with a hot iron or with one of the plastic tapes. A large quantity can be made at once, of course, and divided into the smaller portions. Before using, it is a good idea to stir the mixture lightly.

When everything is ready to go, mix in 1 cup freshly washed and still damp blueberries, carefully stirring until each is coated with flour. Then quickly mix in ⅓ cup cold water to make an easily handled dough. Shape this, with as little handling as possible, into a cake about an inch thick. Dust the loaf lightly with flour, if you have any extra, so it will handle more easily.

Lay the bannock in an already warm frying pan. Hold it over the heat until a bottom crust forms, rotating the pan a little so the loaf will shift and not stick. Once the dough has hardened enough to hold together, turn the blueberry bannock, perhaps using a spatula or a plate and supporting the loaf long enough to invert the frying pan over it, then turning everything together. When it seems ideally browned, test by shoving in a straw or sliver. If any dough adheres, the loaf needs more heat.

Maybe you'd prefer muffins. Then just add 2 tablespoons sugar, 2 well-beaten eggs, and 1 cup milk to the mix and berries. Stir just enough to dampen all the dry ingredients. Fill greased muffin rings, improvised if you want from aluminum foil, about ⅔ full. Bake in a hot oven about 20 minutes. Eat at once.

Blueberry flapjacks are something special. Make the regular batter and drop it, ⅓ cup at a time, on a hot, lightly greased griddle. Sprinkle 2 tablespoons of blueberries over each flipper. When the hot cake starts showing small bubbles and its underside is golden, turn and brown the other side. Have the butter dish loaded and enough syrup ready to match the appetites.

CRANBERRY *(Vaccinium)*

Wild cranberries, regarded by many as the most important berry of the north country, grow along the northern borders of the contiguous forty-eight states and from Alaska to Newfoundland, south to Arkansas and Virginia. Commercial varieties, 60 per cent of which are raised in Massachusetts, are delicious, but the wild varieties have more flavor and color.

Three species of this prime bear food liven bogs, marshes, rocky or dry, peaty, acid soil, and open coniferous woods across this continent, where they are also known as lingenberries, lowbush cranberries, American cranberries, cow berries, rock cranberries, lengon, swamp cranberries, pommes de terre, and partridgeberries.

Although they cling to the vines all winter and when kept fresh by snow are available many months as an emergency food, cranberries are at their best after the first mellowing frost. Many people in the know then pick them by the bushel, often using homemade tooth-edged scoops and then cleaning the loot by bouncing the berries on slanted blankets, as described under blueberries.

CRANBERRY
Left: in flower; *Right:* with fruit.

Wild cranberries vary some, but they are essentially low evergreen shrubs or vines, rising some six inches above the wilderness floor and often growing so thickly that they form lush verdant mats. The leathery green leaves are small, generally rather glossy above, paler and bristled or spotted beneath. The small whitish or reddish flowers, which have four deep petal-like divisions, are attached to the ends of slender stems in such a way that colonists early called the plant craneberry, because the blossoms, which nod when ground winds are blowing, are shaped like the heads and necks of those birds. The name was later shortened to cranberry.

The berries, which are green before they ripen, are edible but unappetizing raw, although, thinly sliced, a few will lend a holiday touch to a green salad. Cooked with enough sugar to mellow their tart acidity, they're an entirely different story. The preserving acidness of the firm fruit, incidentally, has long been one of its most valuable characteristics on this continent, dating from the days when early Massachusetts settlers successfully shipped ten barrels of them across the Atlantic to King Charles II.

They can be stored without preserving, if the fully ripe berries are gathered on dry days and kept in cloth sacks in a cold place. Do not use tight containers, as the cranberries then tend to mold unless kept frozen.

If you're temporarily without handier facilities, it may be valuable, too, to know that wild cranberries can be easily and successfully dried. The best method, although you can improvise, is to strew the fruit on shallow trays that have been lined with cheesecloth and to leave them in a warm place like an attic, or an oven with the door partly open, until they become shell-like and easily mash to a powder. We find this characteristic especially handy in log cabin living. To use these dry berries, just soak them in water and then boil them a few minutes. Add sugar to taste.

There are lots of ways to use cranberries, but our favorite year in and year out, both as a dessert and as a pleasantly pungent supplement to meat, is cranberry sauce. You may have your own method of making this, but with wild berries try stirring 1½ cups of water and 1 cup of sugar together in a saucepan. Bring to a boil and simmer for 10 minutes. Then drop 2 cups of cranberries into the syrup and let bubble until the fruit pops. If someone in the house is trying to lose weight, try cutting the sugar in half and adding instead a level teaspoon of salt.

To serve with your meat for a change, how about a raw cranberry relish that will keep in the refrigerator for weeks? Start by putting 4 cups of cranberries through the meat grinder. Add the pulp and juice of 2 oranges, the chopped rind of 1 orange, the juice of 1 lemon, and 1½ cups sugar. Mix well and allow to stand a day before using for the first time.

Colorful cranberry jelly is always good, and it is very easy to make without failures. Pour ¾ cup boiling water over 2 cups of cranberries in a saucepan and bring quickly to a simmer. After 5 minutes, add ¾ cup sugar and cook another 5 minutes. Then strain, pour into hot sterilized glasses, and seal.

HIGHBUSH CRANBERRY *(Viburnum)*

Despite the name, this shrub of the *Viburnum* family, some twenty species of which occur in the United States, is not a cranberry. A lot of people, too, object to its distinctively

HIGHBUSH CRANBERRY
Top: leaves and fruit; *Bottom:* blossoms.

sweetish-sour odor and flavor. They do at first, that is. It has become one of my favorite berries, especially when I let a few frozen fruit melt on my tongue like sherbet in late fall and winter. I wouldn't swap the provocatively different jelly it makes for any other in the world.

The juicy red highbush cranberries, which often have an

attractive orange hue, are also sometimes called squashberries and mooseberries. They are at their best for cooking just before the first softening frost, although they continue to cling to their stems throughout the winter and are thus one of the more useful emergency foods in Alaska, Canada, and the northern states, where they are to be found usually the year around. Even when soft and shriveled in the spring, they are particularly thirst-quenching, and once you get to recognize the clean but somewhat musty odor, you're never going to get the wrong berry by mistake.

Highbush cranberries grow as straggly or erect shrubs whose slender grey branches are generally all within reach of the average adult. The usually three-lobed leaves, whose edges are toothed, resemble those of the maple. Like those of that familiar tree, they become brilliant in the fall. The berries which are actually drupes, each enclosing a large flattened seed, appear in easily picked groups whose flavor becomes milder as they age.

Now for that beautifully sparkling, salmonish-red jelly of perfect texture and unique flavor! This latter will be improved if the still firm berries are picked before the first freeze, while about half ripe. Bring each 2 cups of these to a boil in 3 cups of water. Mashing them as they cook, simmer for 5 minutes. Then strain. Add ⅔ cup sugar to every cup of resulting juice and bring to a bubble. Then pour into hot, sterilized glasses and seal immediately. A lot of people don't care for this at first, but with repeated samplings, many of them come to agree that there's no other jelly quite as good.

PAPAW *(Asimina)*

This fruit so relished by raccoons and possums, sometimes called "false banana" because of its appearance, is also widely known as "custard apple" in deference both to its deliciousness and its family. Like the highbush cranberry, papaws usually call for an acquired taste. But once you come to like their creamy sweetness, they can become one of your favorite fruits. They are sometimes found in city markets, but they are at their best harvested when ripe, which in the North may mean after the first frost.

This hardy cousin of similar tropical fruits is native from New York southward to Florida and west to Nebraska and Texas. Preferring ground that is moist and fertile, it is most often seen in stream valleys and on the lower adjoining hills. It grows, too, in small clearings and along shaded roadsides. Papaws planted during landscaping often turn out to be doubly valued for their decorativeness as well as for their fruit.

PAPAW
Left: bud and leaf scar; *Center:* branch with flowers and leaves;
Right: fruit.

A big shrub or a small tree, the papaw occasionally grows some forty feet high in the South, with a trunk perhaps as much as a foot in diameter. Northward, however, even the taller trees are often fifteen to twenty feet high, with trunks only a few inches thick. The papaw's large and often drooping leaves, which give it a tropical appearance, are from six to twelve inches long and, growing on short stems, are dark green above and paler beneath.

In early spring, just as these first leaves are starting to open, it blossoms with greenish flowers that later turn to a brownish or reddish purple. Growing from where the branches are met by the stems of the previous year's leaves, these are unusual in that they have six petals in two sets of three. The inner trio bunch together in a little chalice around which the outer three are outstretched like a saucer. About one and one-half inches wide, these produce slender fruits that look like short bananas, from several to about five inches long, with smooth, greenish-yellow hides that become brown a day or two after the papaws are plucked.

Despite the nuisance of several large dark seeds, the papaw has a wealth of bright yellow pulp whose mellow sweetness makes it really something to feast on outdoors, as the hungry members of the Lewis and Clark expedition discovered on their homeward journey. They are quickly gathered, often from the ground. You can also pull them slightly green and put them out of the way in a dark and dry place to ripen.

The custardlike consistency of the ripe fruit, whose odor is also fragrant, blends well with a number of desserts. For 2 people, make a sauce by beating the yolks of 3 eggs briefly, then stirring in 2 cups of milk and ½ cup sugar. Cook in the top of a double boiler until it thickens slightly. Then mix with a cup of papaw pulp that has been strained through a colander. Allow to cool, and then put in the refrigerator. Serve chilled, snowily topped with the beaten whites of 3 eggs into which, after they have become stiff, 6 tablespoons of sugar have been whipped.

Frozen papaw will also make you hope that no unexpected company drops in at the last moment. It's easy to make, although you have to go at it in stages, with everything at the same temperature to begin with. Start by separating 3 eggs.

Beat the yolks until thick, add ½ cup sugar, and whip until creamy. Beat the whites until they form peaks, pour in ½ cup sugar, and continue beating until stiff. Then beat 1 cup of heavy cream until it, too, is stiff. Gently combine all these ingredients and fold in a cup of strained papaw pulp. Then just freeze.

RASPBERRIES and BLACKBERRIES *(Rubus)*

Even expert botanists have trouble trying to tell the numerous members of the raspberry and blackberry family apart. In fact, they can't even agree how many varieties there are in the United States, the estimates varying from about 50 to 390, including the raspberries, the hordes of true blackberries, the cloudberries, baked-apple berries, salmonberries, dewberries, thimbleberries, and a lot more. Me, I don't try to identify them all. I just eat them.

All members of the rose family, these produce closely and deliciously related fruits in commonly varying shades of red, yellowish, and black. Size and softness differ, too, but they are all berries that are made up of many small, generally juicy, pulp-filled ovals, each of which contains a hard seed. They grow over most of the continent, even in the Arctic where their high Vitamin C content is of particular importance. Despite their usually minute differences, they generally resemble market varieties of raspberries and blackberries and are easily recognized by all.

More than one opening day in Maine I've jumped a deer by coming upon a raspberry patch when it was just getting light enough to see. We have to watch the bushes in our yard in British Columbia to see that our horses don't nip them to nothingness. All in all, the *Rubus* family rates at the very top as a summer food for stock and wildlife. Too, the leaves and stems are eaten extensively in the spring, and later on few of the shriveled remains of the berries go to waste.

The tender young peeled sprouts and twigs of raspberries and blackberries are also edible by humans, being something pleasant to chew on when you're in the woods and fields. The leaves provide another of the wilderness teas. You can make a refreshing drink from the ripe berries, too, pressing jars full of them, filling in the spaces with vinegar, and letting stand for a month. Then strain off the juice and seal what you don't use right away in sterilized containers. To serve, sweeten to taste and dilute with iced water.

RASPBERRY
Left: with buds and flowers; *Right:* with fruit.

Besides devouring countless of these raw from the often thorny vines and bushes, we annually enjoy luscious quarts of them with just milk and sugar. But there are other things you can do with these berries which, in dollars and cents, constitute the most valuable wild fruit crop in North America.

Here is a variation of blueberry slump adjusted to raspberries. This recipe can also be used for blackberries and the other varieties by changing the proportions of the sugar and spices according to the natural flavor of the wild fruit.

BLACKBERRY

Mix 1 cup of sugar, 1 tablespoon shortening, ½ teaspoon cloves, ½ teaspoon cinnamon, and 1 tablespoon of cornstarch in a pan. Slowly add 1 cup of boiling water and, continually stirring, bring to a simmer for a minute. Add 3 cups of raspberries to the syrup. While the mixture is bubbling, proceed as in the blueberry slump recipe.

How about an outstanding and easily made pie? Not bothering with a bottom crust, just fill a deep pan with berries that have been mixed with a little flour to absorb the excess juice and thus help to prevent overflowing, as well as to give the syrup more body. Sweeten to taste. Then roll out a pie crust that is thicker than usual, cut this into strips, and crisscross over the fruit. Bake in a moderate oven from forty to sixty minutes or until the crust is golden brown.

These wild berries will speedily cook up into a custardlike dessert that will always be enjoyed whenever it is served. Just stir 4 cups of fruit, ½ cup of hot water, and 1 cup of sugar together in a pan, slowly bringing them to a boil and then briefly simmering until juicy. Moisten 2 tablespoons of cornstarch with twice that much cold water and then about an equal amount of the hot juice. Turn this into the berries and, stirring, let bubble and thicken for 2 minutes. Cool before eating.

Blackberry cordial, which, incidentally, has long been a favorite home remedy for diarrhea, is easy to make when these berries are plentiful. You'll need 8 quarts for this particular recipe, although this latter can be easily halved or quartered. In any event, pick over and wash the blackberries, place in a kettle with 2 quarts of cold water, boil until mushy, and then strain.

For every quart of resulting juice, stir in 2 cups of sugar. Then tie 1 tablespoon each of cloves, nutmeg, cinnamon, and allspice in a cotton cloth. Drop in the juice and boil for 20 minutes. After this has cooled, add 1 pint of brandy or whiskey to every quart of syrup. Pour into sterilized bottles and cork securely. This will mellow with age.

Blackberry wine appeals to some, especially where the bushes are thick with this fruit. After carefully picking over and cleaning a mess of berries, drop them into a crock and crush them thoroughly. Let the mashed berries remain there for a week, stirring them daily. Then strain out all the juice.

For every 3 quarts of juice, use 1 pound of sugar. Boil this with the least amount of water required to dissolve it. Then pour the hot syrup into the juice. Leave in the crock for another full day. Then pour into sterilized bottles or jugs, covering these only with a cloth, as gases will be escaping during the fermentation. When this bubbling process has stopped, taste the wine. If it does not seem sweet enough, add to taste cold sugar syrup, made by slowly simmering 1 cup of sugar in ½ cup of water until syrupy. Bottle.

To avoid possible fines, confiscation, and other difficulties, anyone planning to make blackberry or any other wine from wild edibles or anything else should first inform himself about the rather complicated federal restrictions and regulations. You may do this by writing the Alcohol and Tobacco Tax Division, Internal Revenue Service, U.S. Treasury Department, Washington, D.C. Incidentally, there is a provision whereby, subject to certain limitations, "the duly registered head of any family may, without payment of tax, produce for family use and not for sale an amount of wine not exceeding 200 gallons per annum." There are many local laws, too.

SERVICEBERRY *(Amelanchier)*

Also known as juneberries, the numerous members of this family are used like the blueberries they resemble. Millions were once gathered to flavor pemmican.

Four or five species of serviceberries, which are primarily North American shrubs and trees, are native in the East and up to about twenty in the West. Bearing delicious fruit from Alaska to Newfoundland and south to California and the Gulf of Mexico, they thrive in such habitats as open woods, rocky slopes and banks, and in swamps. Various other common names include saskatoon, shadbush, shadblow, shadberry, sugar pear, and Indian pear. Incidentally, some frontiersmen still make an eyewash from the boiled green inner bark.

One very steep Peace River bank I know, several hundred feet high and a short walk from our British Columbia cabin, was covered with serviceberries. Falls I've counted as many as six black bears eating the fruit on it at once. Then a forest fire burned it off, and the bears don't go there any more. Grouse and pheasant like the fruit and buds, while hoofed browsers, especially mule deer, feed on the twigs and foliage.

The daintily conspicuous, white, longish, five-petaled blossoms appear while the leaves are just expanding and are among the first spring flowers of our native woody plants. They cover the tough, flexible shrubs and small trees which have small alternate leaves, varying from elliptical to almost round, and at least partially toothed. These change from green to a beautiful rusty red in autumn. The loose bunches of berries, whose five-toothed summits cause them to resemble large blueberries, are red when young, becoming purplish or almost black.

SERVICEBERRY
Left: with fruit; *Right:* with flowers.

The sweet juicy pulp surrounds ten large seeds, which add to the flavor when the fruit is cooked. As a matter of fact, although for years I have lived within a few feet of enough serviceberries to supply a good-sized restaurant, I have never much cared for the fruit raw. Cooked, though, especially when the then mild sweetness is enlivened with acid, that's another story. Too, the cooked seeds become even softer and impart an almondlike piquancy to the fruit.

Drying also considerably alters the otherwise somewhat insipid taste for the better. The serviceberries thus treated can be substituted in recipes for currants and raisins. The Indians used to preserve them this way by the thousands of bushels, spreading them in the sun and later beating some of them into a mash which was molded into cakes and dried. The dried berries were also used in puddings and in the famous pemmican which, if you want, you can duplicate today. Essentially, this most nourishing and notable of concentrated outdoor foods is, by weight, ½ well-dried lean meat and ½ rendered fat, both pounded together. Dried serviceberries are mixed in for flavoring.

Today most serviceberries are preserved by canning, and their dark nutty juiciness is invigorating when they're opened in the winter, when maybe snow is whispering on the windows. Bring to a bubble 2 cups of water and 4 cups of sugar. Carefully pour in 6 cups of serviceberries and simmer a minute or 2. Stir in 3 tablespoons of lemon juice. Then pack the hot berries in sterilized pint jars, cover with the hot juicy syrup, and seal. Process the jars 20 minutes covered by boiling water or, if you have a pressure cooker, 10 minutes at 1 pound pressure.

Canned serviceberries make superior pies, although they can also be used fresh for this purpose. For the latter, mix 4 cups of ripe serviceberries with 1¼ cups sugar, 4 tablespoons melted butter or margarine, and 2 tablespoons lemon juice. Bake in a double crust in a moderate oven for 50 minutes or until the crust is a rich brown. The slabs will be runny, and you'll probably have to finish up with a spoon, so serve in deep dishes.

Serviceberry jam is another improvement on the raw berries. Start by putting the washed fruit through a medium-fine food chopper. Then measure 4 cups, add only enough water to cover, and simmer until the berries are tender and pulpy. Add 3 cups sugar, the juice of 2 lemons, the shredded pulp of 2 oranges with all the juice, and the grated rind of those oranges. Let bubble gently half an hour, pour into sterilized jars, and seal.

MAY APPLE *(Podophyllum)*

Springtimes these attractive plants poke up like miniature forests of little opening umbrellas. Preferring moist rich woods and banks, their creamy-white flowers are later familiar from southeastern Canada to Florida and west to Minnesota and Texas. These produce sweetly scented, lemon-yellow fruits which, when delectably ripe, are relished by many.

MAY APPLE
Left: stem with flower and leaves; *Right:* fruit.

This native perennial, a member of the barberry family, is also known as mandrake, wild lemon, and raccoon berry. Only the fruit is edible. The root, which Indians collected soon after the fruit had ripened and used in small quantities as a cathartic, is poisonous. So are the leaves and stems.

Each spring the long horizontal roots, which stay alive year after year, shoot up single-stemmed plants twelve to eighteen inches high. These roots, incidentally, are dark brown, jointed, and very fibrous. Internally yellow, they are mostly about half the size of a finger.

The solitary stems bear either one or two large leaves which open like tiny parasols. It is the latter plants that produce the single flowers which nod on short stems that rise from the fork of the leaves. About two inches wide, these oddly scented blossoms have from six to nine waxy white petals and twice that number of golden stamens.

The sweet yellow fruit, the size and shape of small eggs, ripens from July to September, depending on the climate, generally when the dying plants have dropped to the ground. Despite numerous seeds and a tough skin, it is very enjoyable in moderation raw, although there are those who, as in the case of serviceberries, prefer the May apple cooked.

The raw juice, however, really touches up sweet lemonade and other fruit drinks, while in some parts of the country there are those who add it and sugar to wine.

You can make a luscious, thick, pulpy jam from May apples. Clean about 2 quarts of fully ripe fruit, being sure to remove all stems. Place a layer in the bottom of a kettle. Crush them with a potato masher, repeating this process until all the fruit has been mashed. Add ½ cup water and heat short of simmering for 20 minutes, stirring now and then. Then press the fruit through a colander. To 4 cups of the resulting juicy pulp, add a package of powdered pectin and a pinch of salt. Put back on the heat. When it starts to bubble, stir in 4 cups of sugar. Bring to a full boil, remove from the heat, skim, and seal in hot sterilized jars.

The heat does alter the delicate flavor of the fruit, and although many think this is for the better, there are those who prefer the natural taste of May apples. For these, here is an uncooked jam that will keep for several months in the refrigerator. Clean and crush 2 quarts of ripe May apples as before, add ½ cup water, and heat to lukewarm only—100° F. on your thermometer. Press through a colander. Stir a package of powdered pectin into the still warm juice and pulp and let stand 20 minutes. Add 1 cup light corn syrup to prevent the sugar from crystalizing in the cold. Then thoroughly mix in 4 cups of sugar and a pinch of salt. Pour immediately into sterilized containers and store in the refrigerator.

WINTERGREEN *(Gaultheria)*

These spicy little red berries, which, when very young, I used to pick and eat on a New Hampshire slope slick with pine needles, are the first wild fruit I remember gathering. I still

WINTERGREEN
Left: with flowers; *Right:* with berries.

enjoy both them and the wintergreenish leaves of this small evergreen plant, which is one of the most widely known of all the wild North American edibles. The some twenty-five names accorded it, including teaberry and checkerberry, support this conclusion.

The familiar wintergreen flavor, though, so common to drugstores and markets, is no longer made from this plant, but, when not obtained synthetically, from the distilled twigs and sometimes shreds of bark of the black birch. In older times, quantities of wintergreen were gathered around October, dried, and then packed for shipping. Before the volatile oil was distilled off, they were soaked in water for about twenty-four hours, which will give you an idea if you ever want to make any of your own.

Wintergreens are diminutive members of the heath family, often thriving in the shade of evergreens. A pleasant part of the woods of the Northeast, this midget relative of the salal of the Pacific Coast grows in forests and clearings from eastern Canada to the Gulf states and as far west as the Great Lakes. Western wintergreen, *Gaultheria shallon,* grows on the other side of the continent from California to British Columbia. Although less spicy than the eastern species, the larger and still esteemed berries were highly regarded by the Indians.

The wintergreen is a trail plant whose thin, shrubby stems weave through woodland moss and evergreen needles, sending up from two to six erect branches that are usually less than six inches tall. These bear tiny, frosty, bell-like flowers from June to September. These hang below the small, shiny evergreen leaves which, for the most part, cluster at the tops of the branches. The leaves, whose wintergreen fragrance when crushed makes them unmistakable, are tough when mature, one or two inches long, and oval with little bristling teeth.

The firm berrylike fruit, which is inconspicuous though bright red, can be an important emergency food when found in great enough quantities, as it clings to the stems all winter. It is sometimes seen in the eastern markets and is often turned into pies. The only use I have ever made of these sweetly dry berries, though, has been to enjoy them while hunting, fishing, hiking, or just plain relaxing in the wilderness.

The evergreen leaves are well worth chewing, especially

when young, because of their characteristic flavor and are a food of the ruffed grouse and white-tailed deer. These leaves, when freshly gathered, make a very palatable tea, a teaspoon to a cup of boiling water. Tearing them first into small pieces provides even more flavor, which can be helped along by cream and sugar.

ELDERBERRY (*Sambucus*)

You can use the flowers of the common elderberry in your cooking, feast on the berries, and make flutes from the limbs. As a matter of fact, some Indians knew this member of the

ELDERBERRY

honeysuckle family as "the tree of music" because of the way they made wind instruments from the straight stems. These were cut in the spring, dried with the leaves on, and then the soft pith of their interiors was poked out with hot sticks. In fact, this is a way to make spouts for gathering sap from maples, birches, and other trees.

The common or American elderberry, sometimes known as the sweet elder, is a shrub growing from four to twelve feet high and occasionally in the South reaching the proportions of a small tree. The stems often spring in erect groups from tangled roots in moist, fertile soil along fences, walls, roadsides, ditches, banks, streams, and in fields from the Maritime Provinces to Manitoba and south to Florida and the Gulf of Mexico.

The green-barked stems, the larger of which were sometimes used for arrows, are mostly filled with porous white pith when young, this core becoming smaller with maturity. The bark, too, changes with age, becoming a greyish brown. The opposite leaves are compounded of from five to eleven leaflets, the lower of which are often lobed.

Creamy flat clusters of blossoms, which decorate and pleasantly scent the *Sambucus canadensis* in June and July, are made up of dozens of tiny star-shaped flowers. In late summer and early fall these become juicy, round berries, each with three or four rough seeds.

Quantities of these purplish black berries can be picked in a hurry. But even when at their ripest, they are none too palatable when fresh, although some of the game birds feast on them eagerly. However, there's an easy way to improve the flavor. Just pick and clean the mature berries as usual. Then dry them on trays in the sun or oven or on outspread newspapers in a hot, dry attic. The difference will be astonishing, and this way they will keep well, too.

When you get tired of dried elderberries simmered with a little sugar and lemon to taste, if that ever happens, why not enjoy some of the elderberry pies you may have heard about from your grandmother? A good crust for these can be made by sifting 2 cups flour and ⅛ teaspoon salt together. Cut in

6 level tablespoons butter or margarine. Add 6 tablespoons cold water and mix gently. Roll into a thin sheet and line a heavily greased pie pan. Reroll the remaining pastry for cutting into strips to crisscross over the top.

As for the berries, stew enough of them with a minimum amount of water to fill 4 cups. Then thicken with a little flour to absorb the excess juice and to furnish a thicker syrup. Mix with 1½ cups of sugar, or more, if that doesn't taste sweet enough, and 4 tablespoons of melted butter or margarine. Pour into the shell, cover with the pastry strips, and bake in a preheated moderate oven ¾ hour or until the crust is golden brown.

Or if you'd rather, have a cobbler instead. Mix 2½ cups of dried elderberries, again stewed with a minimum amount of water, 1 cup of sugar, and the juice of 1 lemon. Pour into a greased casserole or deep pan and dot liberally with butter or margarine. Crisscross with pie pastry, made in half amounts from the recipe above, rolled out and cut into strips. Bake in a hot oven, preheated as always, until the crust is brown.

Once you can identify the small white flowers of the common or American elderberry, *Sambucus canadensis,* these showy flat-topped clusters can be washed, shaken dry, stripped from the stems, and beaten in batters that are slightly thinner than usual for pancakes, waffles, and muffins.

You can make elderberry pancakes by sifting together 2 cups flour, 2 teaspoons double-action baking powder, 2 tablespoons sugar, and ½ teaspoon salt. Beat 2 eggs and mix with 2 tablespoons melted butter or margarine and 1½ cups milk. Rapidly combine everything and quickly stir in 1 cup of elderberry flowers. Bake on a hot griddle that has been sparingly greased with bacon rind. Turn each pancake only once, when it starts to make small bubbles, and cook only half as long on the second side. These have a delicate flavor, and even when we have maple syrup, we prefer just butter and sugar on them.

Or if you like fritters, you can dip the entire flower cluster with the tough stem removed into a batter, then fry in deep hot fat until brown. Start the batter by beating 2 eggs, into which stir ½ cup sugar, 1 tablespoon cooking oil, 1 teaspoon vanilla, and 2 cups milk. Sift together 3 cups flour and 5 teaspoons double action baking powder; then beat everything quickly together until smooth. These hot fritters, carefully removed so as not to break the crust and drained on a folded length of paper toweling, are good either plain with the main meal or afterwards with whipped cream.

Elderberries will provide outstanding jelly with the cooperation of an equal bulk of apples, which may be wild, too. Wash these latter and cut them into sections without peeling or coring. Then cover everything with water and simmer until soft, after which mash and strain.

Measure the juice, bring it to a bubble, skim, and add an equal bulk of sugar. Continue boiling until a spoonful falls off the spoon in a sheet. Fill hot, sterilized jelly glasses to within ½ inch of the top. Immediately fill to the rim with paraffin, broken into small pieces and melted over very low heat. Cover with a cloth, cool, label, and then store in dry, cool darkness.

Elderberry wines and cordials have come down through the centuries. They can be readily made by substituting this fruit in the recipes given for blackberries.

STRAWBERRY (*Fragaria*)

Everyone knows the wild strawberry, similar to domestic varieties but usually far smaller and always infinitely sweeter. Some four species sweeten the air from the Arctic Circle to Florida and California, growing wild nearly everywhere except in arid country. Deer like to browse on these juicy members of the rose family, which are found in open woods, fields, clearings, and along dry hillsides and shaded banks, often so abundantly that a few square feet provide a meal.

I personally know of no more delicious berry, wild or otherwise. And those who finally feel the need for something to offset the delicate sweetness can brew strawberry tea, dropping 2 full handfuls of the sawtoothed leaves into 4 cups of boiling water and allowing them to steep for 5 minutes. Too, a refreshing drink can be made from the strawberries themselves by first partially crushing them and then stirring them in cool water.

STRAWBERRY

The stems and stalks of this popular perennial are also tasty. Incidentally, fresh wild strawberries have additional value by being a rich source of Vitamin C, about one-half to two-thirds of a cup equalling the Vitamin C content of an orange.

Recipes for strawberries are legion, but over the hungry years we have found the following 4 to be particularly efficacious with the wild varieties. They are simple. For instance, there's strawberry shortcake. All you need for this tiptop treat is wild strawberries and hot bannock.

To match about 2 quarts of berries, freshly picked and left

standing drenched with a cup of sugar, you'll need for the bannock: 2 cups sifted flour, 2 tablespoons sugar, 2 teaspoons baking powder, 1 teaspoon salt, 4 tablespoons shortening, and ¼ cup cold milk or slightly more.

Sift all the dry ingredients together into a bowl. Work in the shortening; then quickly stir in enough cold milk to make a soft dough.

Knead this dough very briefly on a floured board. Roll it out about ½ inch thick. Lay half of the dough in a greased pan and dot it with chunks of canned butter. Spread the other half on top. If you prefer individual biscuits, just cut the dough into ovals with a floured can top or glass. Baking in a very hot oven takes 12 to 15 minutes.

Afterwards carefully separate the steaming layers, ladle the sweetened berries between and above, and fall to it. Raspberries, blueberries, serviceberries, blackberries, and similar wild fruits are also good with this hot bannock.

The shortcake tastes even better with whipped cream made from evaporated milk. In case you want to try it in the woods sometime, there's a simple gimmick to this. Milk and utensils have to be icy cold. This can be arranged easily enough by submerging bowl, beater, and can of milk in a mountain stream.

So chilled, most evaporated milk quickly whips to about triple volume. A couple of teaspoons of lemon juice, canned or fresh, can be used to increase the stiffness after the milk is partially whipped. Some bush cooks also use an envelope of unflavored gelatin, dissolved in a minimum of water, for this purpose.

How about some wild strawberries fried? Clean 4 cups of fresh strawberries, except for their stems. Chill the berries as much as possible; if you're vacationing, perhaps by partly immersing them in a brook or spring. Keep the berries dry.

For the batter, beat 1 egg with 1 cup milk. Then add 1 tablespoon melted butter or margarine, ⅛ teaspoon salt, ¼ cup sugar, and 1 teaspoon vanilla. Blend thoroughly. Mix 1½ cups flour with 3 teaspoons baking powder. Combine with the egg mixture and beat until smooth.

Hold each chilled berry by its stem and dip carefully into the batter. Then drop into hot deep fat and fry until well browned. This will take about a minute. Save what you don't eat on the spot to mete out, with whipped cream if you have it, for dessert.

Here's an open strawberry pie that will really command attention. To make the 9-inch pie shell, sift together 1 cup sifted flour and ½ teaspoon salt. Cut in ½ cup of shortening. Handling this quickly and lightly, add only enough water, about 3 tablespoons, to make a dough that will hold together when rolled. Roll out and spread on a greased pie pan. Bake in a hot oven for 12 to 15 minutes or until done.

Simmer together 1 cup of crushed wild strawberries, ½ cup sugar, and 2 tablespoons of cornstarch until thick and syrupy. Meanwhile, pack the cooked pie shell with the ripest and juiciest wild strawberries available. Drench them with the hot syrup. Chill and serve.

This pie is delicious, too, when similarly prepared with raspberries, blackberries, and such. Sweetening may be varied to taste.

The cheeriness of homemade wild strawberry jam is especially suited to stormy winter days. For 2 pints, which will go a long way, you'll need 4 cups apiece of sugar and crushed berries. Stir the strawberries, measured after mashing, with the sugar in a large pan. Bring to a boil, continuing to stir until the sugar is melted. Keep at a rolling boil for 14 minutes. Then skim off the white foam and seal in hot sterilized glasses.

CURRANTS and GOOSEBERRIES (Ribes)

Some eighty species of currants and gooseberries grow across the United States and Canada, from Alaska to Labrador southward to North Carolina, Texas, and California. Although differing considerably, they closely resemble cultivated varieties. All produce fruit that is edible raw and particularly when cooked, although the bristliness and odor of some of the berries call for an acquired taste, especially when devoured directly from the bushes.

CURRANT
Left: with flowers; *Right:* with fruit.

Although thriving under varied conditions, especially in the West, they are typical of open, moist places, and they often grow by streams, springs, and bogs. Important Indian foods, they were among those soon adopted by the settlers and frontiersmen.

Double-crust gooseberry pie was famous back in colonial days. Just cream ¼ cup butter or margarine, add 1 cup brown sugar, and blend well. Beat 2 eggs slightly and stir in. Add 3 tablespoons evaporated milk, 2 cups ripe gooseberries, and ¼ teaspoon vanilla. The crust ingredients are the same as with strawberry pie, although in double amounts because of the addition of a top crust. Bake in a hot oven for 15 minutes to seal the crust and deter any running over. Then lower the heat to moderate and bake for 15 minutes more or until the pastry is brown on top. You can make this with ripe currants, too.

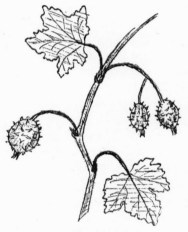

GOOSEBERRY

Gooseberry tarts have long been favorites, and are especially good in cold lunches when you're in the woods. We also make these with currants. In fact, with tarts in particular, we enjoy the varying flavors of the different varieties of gooseberries and currants that grow near our cabin in British Columbia and which are all easily recognizable because of their maple-shaped foliage and their likeness to domestic species.

Just simmer the cleaned berries, with barely enough water

to prevent scorching, until they come apart. Then remove them from the heat, sweeten liberally to taste, and put aside to cool. When they are cool, spoon them into pastry shells made by fitting the aforementioned pie pastry into greased muffin tins. Cover with a top crust brushed with melted butter, and bake in a moderate oven until the crust is nearly done. Remove long enough to brush with beaten egg and then put back in the oven to glaze for 4 minutes. We find these best cold.

Currant wine is simple to make, if the impulse ever seizes you. Wash and clean 10 pounds of currants and pour, along with 5 pounds of sugar, into a 2-gallon crock. Fill the crock to within an inch of the brim with cold water. Then spread cheesecloth across the top and leave in a warm place. For the next 6 weeks, carefully stir the mixture twice weekly. Then strain and allow to stand for an additional 2 weeks to settle. Finally, strain the resulting currant wine and store in sterilized bottles.

We'd rather use any excess currants for jelly which, especially when mixed with a bit of dry mustard, really does things for lamb and venison sandwiches. Mashing 12 cups of ripe clean currants, simmering for 10 minutes in 1½ cups water, and then straining through a jelly bag makes 6 cups of juice. Mix a 3-ounce package of pectin with this while it is still hot and, stirring constantly, add 6 cups of sugar and bring to a full hard boil for a minute. Then take from the heat, skim, and quickly pour into hot sterilized glasses. Immediately fill to the brims with melted paraffin, cover to protect from drafts which might break the glass, and leave to cool. Label and store as usual.

Gooseberry jam is more than worth the trouble. Just clean your berries, cut off the blossom ends, mix with an equal weight of sugar, and let stand overnight. Then bring to a rolling boil, and stirring, let boil for 20 minutes. Skim, pour into hot sterilized jars, and seal immediately.

PARTRIDGEBERRY *(Mitchella)*

Partridgeberries are so easily recognizable that they make a good emergency food. Too, they are available from autumn to spring, clinging conspicuously to the trailing evergreen shrubs throughout the winter. You will find them in moist woodlands and clearings from Nova Scotia and New Brunswick to Florida, west to Minnesota, Arkansas, and Texas. Other names include twin berries and checkerberries.

PARTRIDGEBERRY

We have a single species of partridgeberry on this continent. Another grows in Japan. Ours is a slender, creeping vine, six to twelve inches long, putting down new roots along its prostrate stem. The small, shiny, smooth-edged leaves grow on short stems in opposite pairs. Dark green and sometimes white-veined, they are oval or heart-shaped and usually no more than one-half inch long on average, although they run closer to three-fourths of an inch in some sections.

The June flowers burst out in pairs, often with the past year's coral red berries. These fragrant pairs of half-inch blossoms, each with four pinkish or white petals, grow together at their bases in such a way that it takes two blooms to make one berry. The fruit, too, has a distinctive Siamese-twin aspect.

It ripens during the usual fall hunting seasons, and I often enjoy its aromatic pleasantness while wandering through the woods. Although seedy and on the dry side, it will take the edge off hunger. Ruffed grouse, bobwhite, wild turkey, and small animals including the red fox like it, too.

MULBERRY *(Morus)*

Mulberries ripen in early summer and at this time of the year are one of the favorite foods of songbirds and small game. They are also widely popular in jellies and pies, especially when their sweetness is modified by a touch of lemon. We have gathered them by the gallon for these purposes just by shaking a heavily laden branch over an outspread tarpaulin.

Although up to some dozen species of mulberries are distributed over our north temperate regions, the best of the fruit comes from the native red mulberry. This is a small tree, generally twenty to thirty feet high with a trunk diameter of one to one and a half feet, which prefers the rich moistness of bottomlands and foothill forests but which has been introduced to many yards and streets. A standby of Indians and of early European explorers and settlers, it grows from New England to the Dakotas and south to Florida and Texas, being especially prolific in the Ohio and Mississippi valleys. The soft but tough wood has been used for everything from furniture and fence posts to ships.

The often crooked branches of the red mulberry commonly spread into dense, broad, round domes. These become dark green with sharply toothed leaves, from three to five inches long and almost as wide, which are irregular in shape from their generally heart-shaped bases to their pointed tips. The undersurfaces are paler than the rough tops and often slightly downy. The stems have a milky sap. Incidentally, the twigs are sweetish and, especially when tender in the spring, edible either raw or boiled. The flowers grow in greenish spikes in the joints between leaves and branches.

MULBERRY
Left: winter twig; *Center:* branch with leaves and fruit;
Right: bud and leaf scar.

Despite the name, the ripe fruit of the red mulberry somewhat resembles that of the blackberry in color as well as shape, becoming dark purple when ready to eat. Even though you'll no doubt eat as you pick, you may collect what seems to be an excess. If so, don't overlook the excellence of the juice as a warm-weather drink, either pressing this through cheesecloth or extracting it with an electric juicer. A little lemon juice and sugar, stirred in to taste, will improve the flavor. We like to dilute this juice about half and half with crushed ice.

Mulberry jelly is bright, quivery, and worth the trouble if you live where the berries are plentiful. Mash 4 cups of cleaned fruit in a kettle. Add ¼ cup water. Bring slowly to a simmer, then boil rapidly for 10 minutes. Pour into a jelly bag to drip without squeezing. Add 1 teaspoon of lemon juice to each cup of juice.

Return to the kettle. Stir in 2 cups sugar and a package of pectin, and boil until the juice will fall in a sheet from the side of a spoon. Skim, pour immediately to within ½ inch of the tops of hot sterilized glasses, fill the remaining space with melted paraffin, cover to protect against drafts, and when cool, put away on a dark, dry shelf.

Mulberries and steaming hot dumplings make a happy match. If you're just cooking for 2, ready 3 cups of the ripe fruit. Mix these with 1 cup sugar or, better, sweeten to taste. Add the juice of a lemon. Bring to a simmer in a large pot. When you're ready to sit down to the main meal, drop on a white dome of dumplings and cover tightly.

Enough dumplings for 2 diners are a cinch to make. About 12 minutes before mealtime, mix 2 cups flour, 2 teaspoons baking powder, and 1 teaspoon salt. Work in 2 tablespoons butter, margarine, or other solid shortening. Make a bowl-like hollow in the center. Have everything ready to go, for these dumplings should be cooked and served immediately.

Now pour 1 cup milk into the well in the center of the dry ingredients. Mix quickly and gently with a folding, rather than a stirring or whipping, motion.

Moisten a large spoon in the mulberry juice. Use it to place large spoonfuls of dough, apart from one another, atop the boiling berries. Cover tightly. After several minutes, you may if you want turn each dumpling speedily and carefully. Recover immediately and continue boiling until light and fluffy.

When the dumplings are done, take out and top each with a spoonful of butter or margarine. If any dumplings remain for second helpings, place them in a separate hot dish so they won't become soggy. Spoon the hot berries over the ones you're eating. Pour on some milk or cream if you want. And see what everyone's idea is about dessert for the following meal.

GROUND CHERRY *(Physalis)*

Ground cherries, close relations to the tomato but not even distant cousins of the cherry family, grow in all parts of the

GROUND CHERRY

country except Alaska. Also known as strawberry tomatoes and husk tomatoes, they have long found their way into occasional markets, being raised commercially in some localities. They are also found in fields, waste places, and in open country, but particularly in recently cleared and cultivated ground, where they ripen from July through September.

This rapidly growing annual takes up a lot of room, its single or forked branches many times sprawling over several feet of ground, but it seldom grows more than a foot high. The pointed leaves have broadly and roundly indented edges. The decorative flowers, which make one hardy perennial of the family, the Chinese lantern plant or winter cherry, a flower garden favorite, resemble tiny yellow funnels. Their five petals later greatly expand, completely enclosing the round yellow berry in a tiny papery husk.

These large yellowish coverings so protect the single golden fruits that when, as often happens, they fall early, they still ripen on the ground. Too, if you will store the encased berries dry, they will continue to become more sugary for several weeks. But in some areas you have to beat the game birds and some of the game and fur animals to them.

One of the first pies I ever remember eating was made of ground cherries, and it must have been good to stay in my memory all these years. A bit of lemon brings out the flavor, and a little nutmeg enhances it. Combine 4 cups of cleaned fruit, 1¼ cups sugar, ½ teaspoon nutmeg, 2 tablespoons lemon juice, and 2 tablespoons melted butter or margarine. Pour into an uncooked 9-inch pie shell and top with another thinly rolled sheet of dough, venting this last. Cook in a moderate oven, preheated as always, 45 to 55 minutes, or until the crust is golden. This pie is runny, and you'll probably have to finish up with a spoon, but the flavor is all the better for that.

Ground cherries are very easily put up. Just make a syrup by boiling 6 cups water, 3 cups sugar, and the juice of 3 lemons for 5 minutes. Spoon in enough ground cherries to come to the top of the syrup. Simmer until the fruit is tender and clear, pour into hot sterilized jars, and seal.

The raw berries, which are very refreshing when you're out for the day, make a pleasant dessert with sugar and milk. Or try them with vanilla ice cream sometime. They're good with this, too, after they've been blended as for pie and stewed.

The jam, too, is really scrumptuous. Crush 4 cups of fully ripe fruit, a layer at a time, so that each berry is reduced to pulp. Add 4 tablespoons lemon juice and a package of pectin. Bring the mixture quickly to a boil, stirring occasionally. Then put in 4 cups sugar. Bring back to a hard boil for 1 minute, continuing to stir. Remove from the heat and skim off any foam. Let cool for 5 minutes, stirring occasionally, for better consistency. Then pour into hot sterilized glasses and seal at once as usual.

RUM CHERRY (Prunus)

Some fourteen native species of wild cherries, ranging in size from shrubs to large trees, are widely distributed across the United States and Canada. Game birds and songbirds feast on their fruit summers and falls when it ripens, and even before, and animals feed on the cherries that have dropped to the ground. Deer, elk, moose, and mountain sheep are among those supplementing their diet with the foliage, twigs, and tasty bark of wild cherries. Chipmunks often store large quantities of the seeds for their winter food supply.

The rum cherry, often known as the wild black cherry, is the most important member of the group. This tree is found in woods and open places, particularly along old walls and fences where its seeds have been dropped by birds. The rum cherry is native from Nova Scotia to Minnesota and the Dakotas, south to central Florida and eastern Texas. A slightly different variety grows in the mountain canyons of Arizona and New Mexico.

Rum cherries, sometimes 50 to 60 feet and occasionally 100 feet tall, grow into one of the most highly valued timber trees of the continent. The strong wood, which turns as dark as mahogany upon exposure to air, is popular for cabinet work and for veneering.

RUM CHERRY
Top left: blossom; *Top right:* branch with leaves and fruit;
Bottom: branch with leaves and blossoms.

The bark, pleasantly aromatic with the odor of bitter almonds, is an old-time home remedy for coughs. The reddish, scale-covered outer bark is first removed. Then the greenish layer, best when young and thin, is stripped off and dried. A teaspoon of this is steeped in a cup of boiling water. One or two cupfuls are drunk cold a day, a large mouthful at a time.

The shining leaves of the rum cherry are narrowly oval to oblong lance-shaped, with broadly rounded or wedge-shaped bases and long, pointed tips. Measuring from two to five inches long, and from three-fourths to one and a half inches wide, they have edges that are finely indented with incurving teeth. The short stems, one-half to one inch long, have a pair of reddish glands at their tops.

The long clusters of white flowers start drooping from the ends of branches while the leaves are still growing. The roundish berries ripen to a bright black or dark purple in August and September, varying from tree to tree in size and quality. Their bittersweet, richly winy juiciness, although usually puckery, makes them popular, at least among young boys, wherever they grow.

Rum cherries got their name from being used by old-time New Englanders to mellow rum and other brandies, as well as whiskies. The procedure was to sweeten the strained and simmered juice of crushed rum cherries with an equal bulk of sugar, then add it to taste to the raw liquors. The process was favored because, in addition to its soothing effect, it also thriftily stretched the available supplies of the ardent spirits.

Cherry bounce still works out well with rum cherries, the proportions being 1 quart fruit and ½ pound sugar to a pint of whiskey. Clean and stem the fruit. Start by covering the bottom of a wide-mouthed jar with a thick layer of cherries. Top these with a single layer of sugar cubes. Some connoisseurs then sprinkle on small amounts of clove, cinnamon, nutmeg, and allspice. Continue this process as long as the fruit and sugar last. Then pour in the whiskey. Seal, put away in a dark place, and go about other matters for at least 2 months.

Brandied rum cherries, also popular during the early trading days of New England, can be made by boiling 2 cups of sugar in a quart of water until a clear syrup is formed. Pour this over 2 quarts of cleaned rum cherries and let stand overnight. The next day, drain the syrup into a pot, bring it slowly to a bubble, carefully add the cherries, and simmer for 10 minutes. Then scoop out the fruit with a slotted spoon and pack them into sterilized hot glass jars. Cover them temporarily while boiling the syrup until it is thick. Stir in a pint of rum or other brandy, pour immediately over the cherries, seal, and put away to age.

You can't buy rum cherry sherbet at the store, but you can make a very refreshing version at home. Just squeeze enough ripe cherries to give 2 cups of juice. Bring this to a simmer along with 2 cups of water and 2 cups of sugar. In the meantime, whip the whites of 3 eggs until they are stiff. Pour the hot mixture over these and beat thoroughly. After this has cooled, transfer it to your freezing compartment.

Although they lack pectin, rum cherries make rich dark jelly when combined with apples. The latter should be sour and preferably green. Quarter them whole, put in a kettle with just enough water to cover, and simmer until tender before straining off the clear juice. Mash the cleaned and washed cherries, add ½ cup hot water, and simmer to a pulp, stirring to prevent scorching. Then place in a jelly bag which has been dipped in hot water, and squeeze out the juice. Or you can strain this by pressing the berries in a large sieve lined with facial tissues.

Get 2 cups apiece of both juices boiling together. Then add 4 cups sugar, stirring only until dissolved. Boil rapidly until a large spoon of the mixture runs off in a sheet. Remove from the heat, pour into hot sterilized glasses set on a towel, seal with melted paraffin, cool, and store in a dark, cool, dry place.

Rum cherry jelly can also be made with added pectin instead of apples, and you may very well disagree with us and like it even better. Simmer the crushed ripe berries, which vary quite a bit in juiciness, with ½ cup hot water for 20 minutes and then strain. You'll need 3½ cups of juice.

Return this to the heat, mix in 1 package of pectin, and,

stirring, let come to a boil. Add 4½ cups sugar and, continuing to stir, bring to a full boil for no more than a minute. Remove from the heat, skim, immediately pour into hot sterilized glasses, top at once with melted paraffin, cover, cool, and store as before. Incidentally, any wild jellies that are to be kept in a damp place, or mailed as personal gifts, should be put instead into vacuum-sealed or screw-topped jars.

The rum cherries that grew along the orchard walls of my grandparents' farm in western Massachusetts seemed particularly plump, and when I went there as a boy my Grandmother Adams used to prepare me a special dessert of them. She started this the morning before by pitting a small pail of fruit that I had picked early.

She stewed this awhile with a very little water, sweetened it carefully to taste, and then poured the hot juice and berries over thin slices of bread; first bread, then fruit, then another slice of bread, and so on, finally filling the deep dish with what was left of the fruit. She then covered this and, when it was cool, set it in the ice compartment of her ice box. That night I would enjoy it with fresh thick cream and maybe a little more sugar.

CHOKECHERRY *(Prunus)*

Perhaps the most widely distributed tree on this continent, the chokecherry grows from the Arctic Circle to Mexico and from ocean to ocean. Despite their puckery quality, one handful of the small ripe berries seems to call for another when you're hot and thirsty. The fruit, which is both red or black, also makes an enjoyable tart jelly.

Often merely a large shrub, the chokecherry also becomes a small tree up to twenty-five feet tall with a trunk about eight inches through. It is found in open woods, but is more often seen on stream banks, in thickets in the corners of fields, and along roadsides and fences. Although the wood is similar to that of the rum cherry, it has no commercial value because of its smallness.

CHOKECHERRY
Left: flowering branch; *Center:* branch with leaves and fruit; *Right:* winter twig.

Chokecherry leaves, from two to four inches long and about half as wide, are oval or inversely ovate, with abrupt points. They are thin and smooth, dull dark green above and paler below. The edges are finely indented with narrowly pointed teeth. The short stems, less than an inch in length, have a pair of glands at their tops. The long clusters of flowers blossom when the leaves are nearly grown. The red to black fruits, the size of peas, are frequently so abundant that the limbs bend under their weight.

An attractive and tasty jelly is made by adding 2 parts of cooked apple juice to 1 part of cooked chokecherry juice and proceeding as with rum cherry jelly. Too, a pure version can also be prepared with the help of commercial pectin.

Any of these tart wild cherry jellies can be used to flavor pies. Start by lightly beating 3 eggs. Mix 1 cup sugar, ¼ teaspoon salt, and ¼ teaspoon nutmeg, and add slowly to the eggs, continuing to beat. Melt ½ cup of butter or margarine and add that, too. Then thoroughly stir in 1 tablespoon of your jelly. Pour into an unbaked pie crust, that described under strawberry being excellent. Place in a preheated moderate oven for 10 minutes. Then reduce the heat to slow for 15 minutes, or until it firms.

PIN CHERRY *(Prunus)*

The pin cherry, also known as the fire cherry and the bird cherry, is the only early and light red native wild cherry. Soon dying when shaded, it grows along the margins of woods, in recently burned regions, in clearings, and along fences and roadsides. It is a northern species, ranging from British Columbia to Labrador, south into the high country of North Carolina, Tennessee, and Colorado.

Despite the sourness and the large stones of the small fruit, they are refreshing when you're outdoors and thirsty. When they are brought indoors, it is mostly for making jelly.

The pin cherry, unlike the rum cherry and chokecherry, has its flowers in small, lateral, roundly flat tufts. The thinly fleshed cherries, about one-fourth inch in diameter, grow similarly, on long stems. They ripen during July and August, depending on the latitude, and even before then the birds do not seem to mind their tartness.

The leaves are oblong and shaped like lances, with rounded or wedge-shaped bases and tapering, pointed tips. With edges indented with fine, sharp teeth, they run from three to five inches long and three-fourths to one and one-fourth inches wide. The thin, short stems, again, have two glands at their tops.

The ruddy, shiny brown bark is smooth, or nearly so, on the younger trees. It frequently peels off in horizontal strips to expose a green inner bark that is pleasantly aromatic but exceedingly bitter. Older trees take on a rougher, curlier shagginess. The gum found on the trunks is often enjoyably chewed. Little more than shrubs in the North, pin cherries sometimes grow forty feet or so tall in the southern Appalachians.

PIN CHERRY
Top left: blossoms; *Right:* branch with leaves and fruit.

In some parts of the North, pin cherries are boiled down in a small amount of water, strained, simmered with sugar to taste, and then bottled for use on puddings and pancakes.

Their main fame, though, is as a jelly, and for this their flavor is so fine that there is no need to add any other fruit.

Like other wild cherries, these vary considerably in juiciness and in the amount of pulp. Be sure to crush and simmer enough, with ½ cup water to every quart, to strain out 4 cups of juice. Return this juice to the heat, add a package of pectin, and bring to a boil, stirring. Then mix in 6 cups of sugar and bring to a boil for 1 minute. Remove from the stove, skim, immediately pour into hot sterilized glasses, and seal at once. Cover and cool as usual, then label, date, and store.

My favorite wild cherry dessert today is a deep-dish pie. Moisten 2½ cups juicy pitted fruit with ½ cup water and cook until tender. Add a cup of sugar when almost done. Then pour the hot fruit into a baking dish or casserole.

For the crust, mix 1 cup sifted flour, 1 tablespoon sugar, 1 teaspoon baking powder, and ½ teaspoon salt. Cut in 2 tablespoons shortening. Then quickly stir in enough milk, about ½ cup, to make a soft dough. Spoon this immediately over the fruit. Cut vents. Then get the whole thing at once into a preheated hot oven and bake about 30 minutes, or until the crust is done. Serve hot with vanilla ice cream.

KINNIKINIC *(Arctostaphylos)*

As for kinnikinic, after you have filled up on the sustaining if blandly dry red berries, you can make yourself a smoke with the leaves. Dried and pulverized, these have been a frontier tobacco substitute for centuries. They are both mixed with dwindling supplies of regular tobacco and smoked alone.

The widely distributed and easily recognizable kinnikinic should be better known, if only for possible use as a sustaining emergency food. Some of the other names that have become attached to it are mealberry, hog cranberry, upland cranberry, arberry, and especially bearberry. In fact, one of the best places to look for black bear after they have come out of northern hibernation in the spring is on a sunny hillside patch of kinnikinic.

Kinnikinic is luxuriant across Canada, Alaska, and the tops of Asia and Europe. Preferring a sandy or gravelly upland habitat, this member of the heath family is found south to Virginia, New Mexico, and California. Grouse and other game birds pick its small fat berries. Deer browse extensively on its green, leathery foliage.

KINNIKINIC
Left: with flowers; *Right:* with fruit.

Chinook-bared hills around our log-cabin home are green in the very early spring, while snow is still deep in the woods, because of kinnikinic. This trailing perennial shrub with its long fibrous root forms a dense, matlike, evergreen carpet. The alternate egg-shaped leaves are short-stemmed, small, thick, and tough. The pink flowers, which are inconspicuous, grow like tiny bells that sway in terminal clusters. The sometimes pink berries, which are more often dull red with an orange cast, ripen in the fall.

One of the important things about these berries, especially when considered as potentially important emergency food, is that, hard and dry, they cling resolutely to the prostrate shrubs all winter. Otherwise, although mealy, they are rather tasteless. Cooking improves them considerably, however. Too, people depending on wild fruit sometimes gather them in poor berry years and mix them with blueberries.

The odorless green leaves, gathered in the fall and allowed to dry indoors in moderate heat, make a pleasantly bitter and noticeably astringent tea which is regarded in many parts of the Northern Hemisphere as both soothing to the stomach and tonic. You can make it by covering each tea-spoonful of dried leaves with a cup of boiling water and allowing to steep 5 minutes. One old sourdough I know, though, claims that the best results are obtained if the leaves are first soaked in just enough whiskey to cover them, then measured and timed the same way.

Wild Greens

If you have ever sat down to a well prepared meal that included wild vegetables, maybe you've noticed that many of them seem to taste better than domesticated varieties. I'll let you in on a trade secret. They are better.

Green leafy vegetables, to give just one example, deteriorate very quickly. Even when purchased as fresh as obtainable from the finest nearby market, they'll already have lost a sizeable proportion of vitamins.

Some of the food values of greens diminish as much as one third during the first hour after picking. But gather them fresh from nature's own garden and eat them while they're at their tastiest, and you'll enjoy the best they have to offer.

DANDELIONS *(Taraxacum)*

Gathering wild greens is a happy way to sharpen a satisfactory hunger, even if you go no farther than to collect a bagful of common dandelions. Actually, this familiar vegetable, all too well known because of the way it dots many a lawn, is among the best of the wild greens.

DANDELION

Left: Arctic and alpine dandelion; *Right:* ordinary dandelion.

The well-known dandelion of flower beds, lawns, pastures, meadows, roadsides, and other moist, open places, boasts some three species in this country and about twenty-five in the civilized world, over which it is widespread. The green leaves are long and narrow, spreading in a rosette at the bottom. Their coarse edges, irregularly lobed and toothed, give this wild edible its name, which means "lion's tooth."

The flowers are yellow, maturing into full white ovals of plume-tailed seeds that later scatter in the wind to make dandelions plentiful and persistent. The hollow and leafless flower stems discharge a bitterish milky juice when bruised or severed, as do the roots when the greens are cut free. These roots are generally thick and deep. Such wildlife as mule and white-tailed deer relish the green foliage, while grouse and pheasant find the seeds delectable.

The tender young leaves, available in the early spring, are among the first wild edibles I gather while bear hunting, trout fishing, or just plain hiking or horseback riding through the greening wilderness. At first they are excellent in salads. Later, when the plants begin blossoming, they develop a toughness and bitterness. Changing the first boiling water into which they are crammed will remove much of this bitter taste if you want, but we find it clean and zestful. Incidentally, when you can, include as many buds as possible, as they liven both the color and the flavor.

Young, tender dandelion greens can be used to add character and vitamins to scrambled eggs. Mix 4 eggs and 4 tablespoons cold water with salt and pepper to taste. Add a cup of shredded dandelions. Heat 2 tablespoons of butter, margarine, or bacon grease in a frypan just hot enough to sizzle a drop of water. Pour in the egg and dandelion mixture and reduce the heat. When the eggs have started to harden, begin stirring them constantly with a fork. Remove them while they're still soft and creamy.

Although they contain a laxative, *taraxacum*, the roots, when young, are often peeled and sliced, like carrots or parsnips, for boiling as a vegetable. To remove the characteristic tinge of bitterness, you may choose to change the salted water once. Serve with melting butter or margarine. Being particularly nourishing, these roots are a famous emergency food, having saved people from starving during famines.

Although the woods afford a multitude of teas, they are short on coffees. The dandelion will provide one of these latter. Roast the roots slowly in an open oven all afternoon until, shriveling, they resemble miniature dragons and will snap crisply when broken, revealing insides as brown as coffee beans.

Grind these roots and keep tightly covered for use either as regular coffee or for mixing to extend your normal supplies. Dandelion roots may be used the year around for this purpose. Because I generally roast my grind shortly before freezeup in the fall when the roots are near their strongest, I find I only have to use a level tablespoon of this home-made mixture per cup, whereas I prefer a heaping table-spoon of store coffee.

Dandelion wine is famous. If you'd like to make your own, pick a gallon of the flowers early on a dry morning, making sure that no parts of the bitterish stems are included. Press these into a 2-gallon crock. Pour a gallon of boiling water over them and leave for 3 days. Then strain through a cloth, squeezing all the liquid from the blossoms.

Add the juice and the thinly sliced rind and pulp from 3 oranges and 3 lemons. Stir in 3 pounds sugar. Add 1 ounce yeast. Cover the crock with a cloth and let it stand, out of the way, for 3 weeks while the mixture ferments. Then strain, bottle, and cork or cap tightly.

LAMB'S QUARTER (*Chenopodium*)

In a lot of homes the acknowledged pick of the edible greens is lamb's quarter. The tender tops of this wild spinach, which has none of the strong taste of market varieties, are delicious from early spring to frost-withering fall.

The entire young plant is good from the ground up. Even from the older ones a quantity of tender leaves can usually be stripped. However, the pale green leaves with their mealy-appearing underneaths and the slim stalks are not the only taste-tempting components of this green, also widely known as pigweed and goosefoot.

LAMB'S QUARTER

Indians long used the ripe seeds, 75,000 of which have been counted on a single plant, for cereal and for grinding into meal. These tiny gleaming discs, which develop from elongated dense clusters of small green flowers, are also handy for giving a pumpernickel complexion to biscuits and breads.

Some twenty of the sixty or more species in this genus, which belongs to the same family as beets and spinach, grow in the United States, thriving in nearly every part of the country. Lamb's quarter is a very common annual which grows from two to seven feet tall. By searching, you can usually find plenty of young plants up to about twelve inches high, and these are best for the table. These young plants have a mealy whiteness to them, but they do not require parboiling. Later, the tender tips alone are excellent. The alternate leaves, which are fleshy and tasty, have long stems and angular margins.

Along with other of the more tender leafy greens, lamb's quarter can be given a bit more taste on occasion with the help of a vinegar sauce. Such a flavorful acid also tends to preserve the vitamins C and A in such vegetables. Alkalies, on the other hand, such as the commonly but inadvisedly used baking soda, destroy an unnecessary proportion of these food values.

For 4 cups of loosely packed greens, take 1 small onion, 4 slices bacon, ¼ cup vinegar, ¼ teaspoon salt, and pepper to taste. Shred the greens if they are large. Dice the onion. Mix. Then chop up the bacon and fry it until the bits become brown and brittle. Put in the vinegar, salt, and pepper and bring to a simmer.

You now have 2 choices. You may pour the sauce over the raw greens. Or you may add the greens to the sauce and cook over low heat until they are limp. In either case, serve immediately. And see what the family's idea is for vegetables for the rest of the week.

STRAWBERRY SPINACH (*Chenopodium*)

Strawberry spinach, also known as Indian strawberry and as strawberry blite, is similar to its close cousin, lamb's quarter. The major difference lies in the bright red masses of pulpy fruits which, many a time when I've been moose hunting the Northwest in the early fall, have stained my boots like dye, making this edible easily recognizable. It is common across Alaska and Canada, southward into the northern states.

STRAWBERRY SPINACH

This annual grows upright, with either a single or a branching smooth stem, from several inches to about two feet high. The thin leaves, longer than they are wide, are broadly triangular with wavy or coarsely indented margins. The inconspicuous little flowers grow in the angles between the leaves and the upper portions of the stem, and often in spikes at the top of the stem. They become dense red masses, with the color and softness of strawberries. They are very nutritious, both raw and cooked.

The young stems and leaves, and later the young tender leaves by themselves, may be used like those of lamb's quarter, either raw in salads or cooked like spinach, which they considerably excel in taste, at the same time providing nutritious amounts of vitamins C and A.

PLANTAIN *(Plantago)*

Plantain is almost as good as lamb's quarter. Furthermore, plantain is as well known to most of us as are the similarly prepared and eaten dandelions, although not usually by name.

PLANTAIN

It is the short, stemless potherb whose broadly elliptic green leaves rise directly from the root about a straight central spike. This singular spike blossoms, although possibly you've never noticed it, with minute greenish flowers that later turn into seeds. At any rate, plantain is found all over the world, even growing through sidewalks in New York, San Francisco, and Boston.

Some nineteen kinds of plantain thrive in the United States. One of the more widely distributed of these is the seaside plantain, also known as goosetongue, which grows along such widely separated coasts as those of Quebec, Nova Scotia, New England, Alaska, British Columbia, and California. The natives in Alaska boil this fresh both for eating on the spot and for canning for winter.

Plantain leaves make excellent greens. Fact is, the greener they are, the richer they are in vitamins A and C and in minerals. They are good boiled. What holds for plantain, when it comes to this common if often murderous method of cookery, goes for the other wild greens as well. Unless it means standing over a riled cook with a cleaver, try to see that all these are cooked only until just tender and still slightly crisp. This usually takes a surprisingly brief time.

The simple gimmick with these wild vegetables is to start them in a minimum amount of boiling water and to cook them, covered, as rapidly and briefly as possible. Young plantain and such can be lifted directly from the rinse to the saucepan and cooked without added water.

For two liberal servings of slightly older greens, ½ cup water and ½ teaspoon salt will do the job. When the greens become tougher, a full cup of water may be required. Any of the vitamin- and mineral-rich fluid remaining should be used, as in soups, gravies, sauces, and the like, unless there's some reason against this such as unusual bitterness. Me, I drink it.

Plantain, also called ribwort and soldiers herb, is mildly astringent. During pioneer times, and even today in some backwoods localities, the fresh leaves are mashed and applied to cuts, scratches, and wounds. The leaves are also used for tea, ½ handful being dropped into a cup of boiling water and allowed to steep for ½ hour.

SOW THISTLE *(Sonchus)*

This very well-known weed, introduced from Europe where it is used as a potherb, has become common throughout most of the cultivated regions of the world including those of

SOW THISTLE

North America. It is so familiar, as a matter of fact, that the tendency is to disparage it. However, in parts of California where dandelions are largely absent the similar sow thistle can be used as an early season green in place of these favorites.

Nearly everyone knows this thistle with the prickly or

bristly but otherwise dandelionlike leaves, best handled with gloves, which grows close to civilization. Its top clusters of yellow flowers resemble those of the dandelion but are much smaller. They later develop a multitude of seeds that are one of the favorite foods of goldfinches, those cheerful little cousins of pet canaries.

Like the dandelion, the sow thistle is characterized by a milky sap. This sap is bitterish, again like that of the dandelion, and this is a reason why some users prefer to boil the leaves in two changes of salted water. Even when we gather the smaller of these succulent green leaves as late as midsummer, cutting them off close to the thick stalks so they can drop unhandled into a bag, we personally relish this slight bitterness, however. We just drop them into a small amount of boiling salted water, cover, cook very briefly only until tender, and eat hot with melting butter or margarine or, for second choice, with oil and vinegar.

If you catch the leaves young enough, they make a tasty salad along with sliced tomatoes and hard-boiled eggs. For a really top dressing for this, dissolve ½ teaspoon salt in ¾ cup olive or salad oil. Stir in ¼ teaspoon pepper. Then whip. Keep in a bottle in the refrigerator and shake vigorously before using. A way to change the taste at times, particularly effective with this salad, is by beating 1 tablespoon crumbled Roquefort cheese into 4 tablespoons of the dressing.

PURSLANE *(Portulaca)*

Purslane, although commonly unnoticed except as a weed, is sometimes the tastiest crop in the home gardens where it widely occurs. This annual also frequently becomes troublesome in fields and waste places throughout the contiguous forty-eight states, in the warmer parts of Canada, and even in Mexico where it is sold in the markets.

The reason for this distribution, which is worldwide, is its tremendous production of seeds, relished by birds and rodents. Although purslane does not become large, 52,300 seeds have been counted on a single plant. Indians in our Southwest used these for making bread and mush.

The trailing, juicy plant which is familiar to almost everyone who has ever weeded a yard, is native to India and Persia where it has been a food for more than 2,000 years. An early mover to Europe, it has been eaten there for centuries. Introduced to the New World back in colonial days, it has spread into almost every American city and town.

"I learned that a man may use as simple a diet as the animals, and yet retain health and strength. I have made a satisfactory dinner off a dish of purslane which I gathered and boiled," Henry Thoreau noted in Massachusetts over a century ago. "Yet men have come to such a pass that they frequently starve, not for want of necessaries but for want of luxuries."

The semisucculent purslane, also sometimes called pusley, prefers fertile sandy ground over which it trails and crawls, sometimes forming mats. It seldom reaches more than an inch or so into the air, although it often spreads broadly. The jointed stems, purplish or greenish with a reddish tinge, are fleshy and forking. The narrow, thick leaves, scattered in nearly opposite positions, grow up to about two inches long.

Unfolding their six or seven petals and some eleven stamens only on bright mornings, the small yellow flowers peek out from stems lifting from the forkings of the stalk. They produce tiny round seed vessels whose tops, when ripe, lift uniquely off like lids.

There's a trick, incidentally, to gathering purslane for the table. If you'll just nip off the tender leafy tips, they'll rapidly sprout again. This way just a few plants will furnish you with greens from late June until frost.

Purslane makes excellent salads. However, after its usual grittiness is removed by washing, it has most frequently been enjoyed as a potherb wherever we've lived. Just drop it into salted boiling water, simmer for about 5 minutes or until tender and serve with melted butter or margarine. A little purslane goes surprisingly far, as it loses little bulk in cooking.

You can capitalize a little more on its mildly acid taste, though, by first cutting 4 slices of bacon into small shreds and frying them until crisp. Then pour in ½ cup vinegar and ½ cup hot water, along with 2 teaspoons brown sugar and salt and pepper to taste. Mix these thoroughly, bring to a bubble, and pour over a large heap of tender young purslane tips. Fork the greens gently about until they are all well coated. Garnish with chopped, hard-boiled eggs, sprinkled with paprika.

Individuals who don't like okra frequently object to purslane's mucilaginous quality, which can be an advantage, however, for lending consistency to soups and stews. It can be counteracted, on the other hand, by rolling each young tip, still slightly damp from washing, in flour, then dipping it in beaten egg, and finally rolling it in bread crumbs. Fry in deep, hot fat for about 8 minutes, or until brown.

People who like pickles may be interested to know that purslane has been furnishing these for centuries. As might be expected, methods have varied widely over the years, but you won't go far wrong by just substituting tender young purslane stems for cucumbers in your favorite recipe.

Here's one that works well. Mix 1 cup salt, 2 cups sugar, and 1 cup ground mustard. Gradually moistening and vigorously stirring at first, mix with 2 quarts vinegar. Pour over as many freshly picked and washed young purslane stems as it will cover. If you have a large crock, fresh purslane and pickling brine may be added day by day until the crock is full. Then cover with a weighed-down plate and leave for at least several weeks. These really stimulate enthusiastic conversation when friends stop by.

SCURVY GRASS *(Cochlearia)*

Scurvy has gathered more explorers, pioneers, trappers, and prospectors to their fathers than can ever be counted, for it is a debilitating killer whose lethal subtleties through the centuries have too often been misinterpreted and misunderstood.

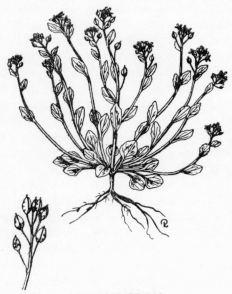

SCURVY GRASS
Bottom left: seed pods; *Right:* entire plant with flowers.

Scurvy, it is known now, is a vitamin-deficiency disease. If you have it, taking Vitamin C into your system will cure you. Eating a little Vitamin C regularly will, indeed, keep you from having scurvy in the first place. Fresh vegetables and fruits will both prevent and cure scurvy. So will the long misused lime juice and lemon juice but, no matter how sour, only if they, too, are sufficiently fresh. The Vitamin C in all these is lessened and eventually destroyed by age, by oxidation, and incidentally, by salt.

Scurvy grass, of which there are several species belonging to the *Cochlearia* family, was one of the first wild greens used by frontiersmen, explorers, and gold diggers across the northern portions of this continent from Alaska to Newfoundland to combat scurvy; hence the name. It so happens, too, that other greens throughout the New World have been similarly used and similarly named, this being one reason for the use of distinguishing Latin names in this book.

This widely distributed scurvy grass, which has the strong horseradishlike odor and flavor of cress, has small white flowers whose 4 white petals are arranged in a cross. These grow in long clusters atop branching stems, a few inches high, that rise from grouped leaves. These delicate little blossoms produce flattish, oval pods that become filled with seeds.

The lower leaves, shaped like broad-based spoons up to about an inch long, group together in narrow rosettes. Fleshy and nearly veinless, they have both smooth and toothed edges. These lower leaves have short thin stems, whereas the upper leaves grow directly from the stalks.

Scurvy grass is not only succulent in spring and early summer, but young lower leaves can also be found in the fall. Although it has a distinctive deliciousness whether eaten raw or after being briefly simmered in a small amount of water, scurvy grass furnishes the utmost in nourishment when served in salads or eaten raw between slices of buttered bread. Or for something really different, spread the bread with cream cheese.

Raw young scurvy grass combines well with freshly cooked white rice. Mix 2 cups cooled rice with the juice of a whole lemon, a tablespoon of olive oil, and salt and pepper to taste. Stir in a cup of scurvy grass leaves that have been torn into fine pieces.

Or try this version. Mix 2 cups hot cooked rice with 2 tablespoons melted butter or margarine and 1 tablespoon

powdered parsley. Add 1 cup shredded scurvy grass. Season
the savory result with salt to taste and serve.

Scurvy grass is also good by itself in a salad, especially
when topped with a dressing made of olive oil, vinegar, salt,
and pepper. Dissolve ½ teaspoon salt in 4 tablespoons of malt
or tarragon vinegar, blended half and half if convenient.
Drop in ¼ teaspoon of preferably freshly ground pepper
and stir well. Then whip in ¾ cup olive oil. Shake vigorously
each time before using.

ROSEROOT *(Sedum)*

Roseroot is another of the wild greens that is known as
scurvy grass because of the often life-saving amounts of
Vitamin C it has provided for explorers, trappers, prospectors,
sailors, and other venturers on this continent's frontiers. It
is also sometimes known as stonecrop and rosewort. Seen in
rocky ground, on cliff walls and ledges, in damply rich
mountain soil, and on the vast northern tundras, it may be
found from Alaska and British Columbia across Canada to
Labrador and Newfoundland, south to North Carolina.

Easy to recognize, it becomes unmistakable when you
scrape or bruise the large thick roots, as these then give off
the agreeable aroma of expensive rose perfume.

The numerous stems of roseroot grow from four to six
inches to about a foot high. They are thick with fleshy leaves,
ranging in color from pale green to pinkish, that are either
oblong or oval, smooth-edged or toothed. Dense tufts of
reddish purple to yellow blossoms crowd the tops of the
stems. Up to about two inches broad, these are composed of
dozens of little flowers, each of which has four petals. These
blossoms produce red and purple seed-filled capsules that
have four or five prongs.

Good from summer to fall, the perennial roseroot and some
of its close cousins are relished both in North America and
in Europe as a boiled vegetable and as a salad plant. The suc-

culent young leaves and stems, which are at their tenderest
before the plants flower, become pretty tough by the time the
seed vessels appear.

ROSEROOT
Bottom left: root; *Right:* stems, leaves, and flowers.

But then, where the plants are abundant, you can boil
up a feed of the big rough roots, season them with butter
and pepper and a little salt, and enjoy them with your meat
or fish. When they are young, the juicy stems with the leaves
attached lend pleasant overtones to other wild greens, both
raw and cooked.

GLASSWORT (*Salicornia*)

Also called beach asparagus, glasswort bears the additional
names of chicken claws and pickle plant. It is also known
on this continent as samphire because of its use for pickles,
as is a similarly named coastal plant in Europe.

At least four species grow in saline regions from Alaska and

Labrador southward along the Pacific and Atlantic Coasts and around the Gulf of Mexico. Typical of shores, brackish marshes, and glistening tidal flats, these members of the beet and spinach family also pop up on the alkaline mud flats rimming western lakes. All in all, they thrive in salty surroundings, taste salty, and appropriately are also called saltworts.

Because the raw tops remain tender and tasty from spring until fall, and especially because these wild edibles are so very easy to identify, the glasswort can be a life-saving food in an emergency. Canada and snow geese nibble on its greenness early in the season, while in the fall pintails and other ducks seek the seed-rich tips, even though these have reddened with age.

These fleshy, somewhat glassy cousins of lamb's quarter have apparently leafless stems, generally branching from near the base, that are juicily green in summer. As cold weather approaches, however, they redden from the ground up. The stems ascend in series of very noticeable joints, where what are actually leaves appear as minute scales which conceal the even less evident flowers and later the seeds.

Glasswort is particularly delicate when it pokes up early in warm weather in beds of bright green shoots only a few inches tall, although the distinctively briny tops will do a lot for a salad until frost-withering fall. It is both good alone, served with a spicy but not salty dressing, and chopped up with other greens. Salt should be added very discreetly. It is pleasant to chew while walking, unless drinking water is far away.

For some, it loses its singular sprightliness when cooked as a potherb, although this is done in Europe. To prepare it this way, just drop it in boiling fresh water, letting it provide its own salt, and simmer for 5 minutes or until thoroughly tender. Melt butter or margarine over the individual servings.

There are several ways of making glasswort pickles. You can boil young portions of the stems and branches in a very small amount of fresh water until a fork slips through them easily. Then transfer them to jars and cover them with cider or white wine vinegar that has been spiced to taste by boiling it no more than 6 minutes with a large grated onion, a kernel of garlic if desired, and a tablespoon apiece of nutmeg, cloves, and allspice. Seal and let stand for a month.

Or if the glasswort is tender enough to begin with, gather it in the proper lengths, clean, and stack directly in the jars. Make the same spiced vinegar as before, and while it is still bubbling, turn it to overflowing over the greens. Seal as before and let stand for at least a month before sampling. If you find you can spare enough of these for company, they make conversation-stimulating hors d'oeuvres.

WILD CUCUMBER *(Streptopus)*

Wild cucumber, also known as liver berry and twisted stalk, thrives across the northern part of the continent and is common around our cabin in British Columbia. The fresh young shoots impart a cucumberlike taste to a mixed salad, real cucumbers generally being scarce commodities in the wilderness.

This perennial has branched stems which grow up to about four feet tall. The green leaves, which clasp alternate sides of the stem, have parallel ribs and are thinly longer than they are broad, being widest near their bases. The single pinkish or greenish flowers, shaped like tiny bells, droop from minute stalks growing from the junctures of the leaves and the stems.

They become small pulpy berries that, when ripe, range in color from whitish yellow to orange and scarlet. When parched from hunting in Maine and New Brunswick, I've sometimes let one or two linger refreshingly in my mouth.

However, despite their deceptive cucumberlike flavor, they should be used sparingly, as they are cathartic. For this reason, they are known as scoot berries in some localities.

WILD CUCUMBER
Left: branched stem with fruits and flowers; *Right:* young shoots.

Wild cucumber salad is something we like on hot spring days. Shred tender young wild cucumber shoots and leaves into very small pieces, enough to fill 4 cups. Pile these loosely into a bowl and cover with very thin slices of a large sweet onion. Pour a heaping cup of sugar over everything, stir well, and allow to stand in a cool place. Then add ¼ cup of preferably mild vinegar, salt and pepper to taste, and serve.

The young plant is tasty, too, with gelatin. Add a cup of boiling water to the contents of a package of lemon Jello. Stir until completely dissolved. Then pour in a cup of cold water and start to chill. When it has started to set, mix in 1 cup finely shredded young wild cucumber, 1 teaspoon grated onion, ½ cup mayonnaise, and salt and pepper to taste. This may be poured into individual molds or spooned, when set, from a bowl. It goes well with a savory catch of sizzling fish.

NETTLES *(Urtica)*

Don't overcook your wild vegetables. Even with such a formidable green as young nettles, which, like prickly pears, are best gathered with leather gloves and a knife, once the salted water has reached the boiling point and the dark green nettles have been dropped in, they'll be tender almost immediately and ready for that crowning pat of butter or margarine as soon as they are cool enough to eat.

Nettles, which regrow in the same places year after year across Canada and the states, are for the most part erect, single-stemmed greens which sometimes grow up to seven feet tall. The opposite leaves are coarsely veined, egg-shaped to oblong, with heartlike bases, and roughly and sharply toothed. Both stem and leaf surfaces bristle with a fuzz of numerous, fine prickles containing irritating formic acid. Very small green flowers, which, like those of plantain, are easy to overlook, appear in multibranched clusters between leaves and stalk.

Nettle leaves may be gathered in the spring and early summer. These unlikely but delectable edibles are among the first wild vegetables available near our log cabin when greenery begins thrusting up like spring fire, but even so early in the season the presence of stinging bristles makes it necessary to wear gloves while harvesting them. If the skin should be irritated, maybe at the wrists, alcohol can be administered. The Indians of southeastern Alaska, several hundred miles west of our homesite, relieve the stinging by rubbing the irritated skin with the dryish, rusty, feltlike material that covers young ferns or fiddleheads.

NETTLE

When young, nettle leaves and the small entire plants quickly lose their stinging properties when boiled. They have such a delicate flavor that they are good by themselves. Topped with butter or margarine, they are far more subtly delicious than spinach and are excellent sources of vitamins A and C and some of the minerals.

Because they are so easily and positively identified, nettles may be an important emergency food. Too, in a pinch, the stems of the older plants will yield a strong fiber, useful for fish lines.

CLOVER *(Trifolium)*

Everyone who as a youngster has sucked honey from the tiny tubular florets of its white, yellow, and reddish blossoms, or who has searched among its green beds for the elusive four-leaf combinations, knows the clover. Some seventy-five species of clover grow in this country, about twenty of them thriving in the East.

CLOVER

Clovers, which are avidly pollinated by bees, grow from an inch or so to two feet high in the fields, pastures, meadows, open woods, and along roadsides of the continent. Incidentally, when introduced into Australia, it failed to reproduce itself until bumblebees were also imported.

The stemmed foliage is usually composed of three small leaflets with toothed edges, although some of the western species boast as many as six or seven leaflets. This sweet-scented member of the pea family provides esteemed live-stock forage. Red clover is Vermont's state flower. White clover is all the more familiar for being grown in lawns. Quail are among the birds eating the small, hard seeds, while deer, mountain sheep, antelope, rabbit, and other animals browse on the plants.

Bread made from the seeds and dried blossoms of clover has the reputation of being very wholesome and nutritious and of sometimes being a mainstay in times of famine. Being so widely known and plentiful, clover is certainly a potential survival food that can be invaluable in an emergency.

The young leaves and flowers are good raw. Some Indians, eating them in quantity, used to dip these first in salted water. The young leaves and blossoms can also be successfully boiled, and they can be steamed as the Indians used to do before drying them for winter use.

If you're steaming greens for 2 couples, melt 4 table-spoons of butter or margarine in a large, heavy frypan over high heat. Stir in 6 loosely packed cups of greens and blossoms, along with 6 tablespoons of water. Cover, except when stirring periodically, and cook for several minutes until the clover is wilted. Salt, pepper, and eat.

The sweetish roots may also be appreciated on occasion, some people liking them best when they have been dipped in oil or in meat drippings.

Clover tea is something you may very well enjoy. Gather the full-grown flowers at a time when they are dry. Then further dry them indoors at ordinary house temperatures, afterwards rubbing them into small particles and sealing them in bottles or jars to hold in the flavor. Use 1 teaspoon of these to each cup of boiling water, brewing either in a teapot or in individual cups, as you would oriental tea.

MUSTARD *(Brassica)*

Mustard, which flourishes wild over most of the globe, is universally recognizable because of its brilliant yellow flowers that become almost solid gold across many a field and hillside. Five species are widely distributed over the United

MUSTARD

States. Most important of these is black mustard, an immigrant from Europe and Asia, which has become so much at home on this continent that it now grows over most of the United States and southern Canada.

This annual ordinarily grows from two to six feet tall, although in California I have seen it as tall as a telephone pole. A relative of cabbages, turnips, cauliflowers, radishes, brussels sprouts, and similar cultivated vegetables, black mustard grows erect with widely spreading branches. The leaves on the young plants, which are the ones to pick, are rather fuzzy and feel stiffly hairy. The finely toothed lower leaves are deeply indented at the bases of the stalks and less indented as they ascend. These lobes do not appear on the upper, small, extremely bitter leaves that grow, nearly stemless, from the flower stalks.

The sunny yellow flowers are small but numerous. Typically for mustard, each has four petals and six little upright stamens, four long and two shorter. The blossoms mature during the summer into small, short pods. These are filled with dark, minute, zestfully pungent seeds.

One way this pleasantly edible plant can really start the mouth tingling is in a cream of wild green soup—especially when you come in dehydrated from a day of fishing or spring bear hunting and get that first sniff of it, all steaming and savory. To go with 2 cups of chopped or scissored young mustard greens, start slowly heating a quart of milk, not allowing it to boil.

Meanwhile, melt 2 tablespoons of butter, margarine, bacon drippings, or any other edible fat in a saucepan over low heat. Gradually stir in 1½ teaspoons salt, ⅛ teaspoon pepper, and 2 tablespoons flour. Add a finely minced small onion. Then pour in the hot milk bit by bit. Cook gently for 5 minutes.

Drop in the greens and, stirring occasionally, continue to heat just below the boiling point until these are just tender. To be at its best, mustard requires more cooking than most greens, something like a half hour. You'll need a lot, too, as it shrinks considerably. When the soup is ready, sprinkle with paprika. Serve at once.

Mustard, whether used in soup or elsewhere, is most agreeable when it first appears. The young stalks are not hard to identify, particularly as older mustard is often standing in the same patch. The slightly peppery young leaves are enjoyable raw. So are the young flowers with their then subtle pungency. The entire young plant goes well cooked with fish and meat.

Later on, the profusion of golden flowers can be capitalized upon to make a broccolilike dish. When you pick these over, it is best to eliminate any of the small upper leaves because of their bitterness. The blossoms boil up quickly in salted water. Bring them to a rapid boil, then let them stand away from the heat, tightly covered, for 5 minutes. Drain, spread with melting butter or margarine, and sprinkle with a little vinegar. Besides being colorful and delicious, this repast is full of vitamins and protein.

The easily gathered seeds of wild mustard, even after it has grown old and tough, are hard to equal for garnishing salads, adding to pickles and such for that extra seasoning, giving a final authority to barbecue sauces, and lending a wisp of zip and zest to stews. Mustard's very name comes from its seeds, being a corruption of must seeds, which harks back to ancient Roman-occupied Britain, where these were processed by saturating them in a solution of grape juice, or *must*, as it was sometimes called.

Table mustard can be made by finely grinding wild mustard seeds, between two stones, if you're in camp, or in the family food chopper, if you're at home, and adding enough water or vinegar to make a paste. After that, it's up to you. Commercially prepared condiments often contain such additional ingredients as flour, salt, turmeric, and other spices. If you choose to modify your raw mustard with up to an equal bulk of flour, brown this latter slowly and lightly in an oven first to take away the starchy taste. The vinegar may be diluted, depending on its strength, up to half and half with water. Occasionally, the blender likes the added flavor of horseradish. This white-flowered member of the mustard family, with the pungent white roots, likewise grows wild.

A lot of us remember, back when we were growing up, the application of mustard plasters to cold-congested chests and sore backs. These famous old remedies, still highly regarded in many households, can be easily homemade. Just mix ground mustard seeds with an equal bulk of ordinary flour, then stir in enough tepid water to make a paste. Sandwich this sparingly between two cloths and tape into position while still warmly wet. Leave some 20 minutes, or until the recipient, with skin that starts to redden in about 5 minutes, begins to complain too vociferously of the increasing warmth.

WATER CRESS *(Nasturtium)*

Water cress grows over much of North America. Available the year around except when the waters in which it flourishes are frozen, this has long been used in many lands and is cultivated here and in Europe. That which I have seen in markets has been comparatively expensive.

Water cress prefers clean cold water, but with civilization spreading the way it is, you can't always be sure that those streams, pools, wet places, and even springs are not contaminated. A reasonable precaution is to soak the well-washed leaves and tender shoots, including those from the store, in water in which a halazone tablet or so has been dissolved, using two of the little pills to a quart of water and letting stand a half hour. Halazone may be very inexpensively obtained from almost any sporting goods or drug store. These minute tablets work by releasing chlorine gas and therefore should be fresh. A bottle of 100 usually sells for less than 50¢ and should be kept tightly closed in a dark, dry place.

Be sure, too, that you are just gathering water cress, as

the poisonous water hemlocks, which somewhat resemble the carrot plant but with taller stems whose lower leaf stalks have three primary forkings, often grow nearby. The familiar edible, rooting at its stem joints, usually sways and floats in the water. However, it is sometimes found creeping at the edges of cold brooks and springs.

WATER CRESS

The glossy green leaves grow with three to nine segments, the biggest of which is at the base. The minute white flowers blossom on a succession of tiny stems attached to a longish stalk. They produce needlelike pods up to about an inch long which, if tender to the bite, are tasty, too. Gatherable wherever it can be reached, the whole plant has the characteristic peppery flavor of mustard, to which family it belongs.

Although water cress is good both cooked and in its native state, we prefer it raw. However, there is generally plenty where it grows, and it cooks up admirably either by itself in a small amount of boiling salted water or mixed tastily with blander greens.

You owe it to yourself, too, to try it with scrambled eggs. To every 2 eggs to be scrambled, add 2 tablespoons cold water, ¼ teaspoon salt, and ½ cup chopped water cress. Beat well together. In the meantime, be heating 2 tablespoons butter or margarine in a frypan just hot enough to sizzle a drop of water. Pour in the egg mixture and reduce the heat. When the eggs have started to harden, begin stirring them constantly with a fork. Remove while they're still creamy and soft.

Water cress soup is also memorable. For one variety which we have found to be exceptional, heat 3 cups fresh milk with 1½ teaspoons salt. In the meantime, run enough cold water cress through the meat grinder to fill 1 cup. Add this to the hot milk and simmer 5 minutes, keeping the pan covered as much as possible. Just before sitting down to eat, beat until smooth and add 1 cup of fresh milk or cream. Serve as soon as heated thoroughly, topped with sprinkled paprika and fresh sprigs of cress.

There's a wonderful way out if someday you make too much green salad, predominated by water cress and liberally dressed with oil and vinegar. Empty a can of mushroom soup into your blender along with the salad and dressing and end up with a thick puree. Let this simmer an hour in the top of a double boiler, stirring it occasionally. You may have to vary the fluid content to obtain the desired thick soup. Decorate this with vitamin-teeming paprika.

Water cress will also somewhat similarly solve the problem of leftover cooked partridge or chicken. Cut up 2 cups of the meat and drop it into your blender, along with 1½ cups of the broth, 2 cups water cress, and 2 cups light cream. Run at top speed until you have a smooth liquid. Once more, heat this in the top of a double boiler, salting it to taste. Sprinkle with paprika and serve hot.

The succulent shoots and tender leaves of water cress have made it a favorite garnish and salad staple since olden times. In fact, the flavor of nearly every salad can be enhanced by the addition of this edible. Too, water cress is famous sandwich fodder, either plain or chopped and blended with chopped hard-boiled egg. As if that weren't enough, you can make a nutritious tea by steeping a teaspoonful of the mineral-swarming leaves or roots in a cup of boiling water.

SHEPHERD'S PURSE (Capsella)

Shepherd's purse is valuable to wild food seekers in that it is one of the more common of the wayside weeds, being found throughout most of the year in gardens, lawns, vacant lots, cultivated fields, and paths throughout most of the world where civilization has moved. It is quickly recognizable, and the tender young leaves, which, like others of the mustard family, are pleasingly peppery, may be enjoyed either raw or cooked. Indians even made a nutritious meal from the roasted seeds.

This wild green is familiar because of its flat triangular or heart-shaped seed pods which, their broad bases uppermost, ascend the top parts of the stalks on short stems. A favorite food of blue grouse, these diminutive pouches develop from long clusters of tiny white flowers, each with twin pairs of opposite petals. Long green leaves, both smooth-edged and roughly toothed, grow in a rosette near the ground.

Growing so near to the earth and in such accessible places, these leaves are apt to pick up a lot of dust and grit, so it is best to gather them young and then wash them well, afterwards drying them in a towel. Otherwise, the dressing will slip off and form a pool in the bottom of the salad bowl. Tear, don't cut, these greens into bite-size pieces and toss them lightly with enough oil and vinegar, mixed 4 parts to 1, to coat them thoroughly. Arrange contrasting red tomato slices for trim. Incidentally, these tomatoes tend to become too watery if tossed with the greens. Serve without delay.

SHEPHERD'S PURSE
Top: stalks with leaves and flowers; *Bottom:* rosette.

These young greens, which vary considerably in size and succulency according to the richness of the soil where they grow, can also be carefully gathered, washed, and then placed in a frypan where a little bacon has been cut fine and partly fried. Some sour cream is added, but the cooking is slight; just enough to wilt the leaves. Spoon out hot and divide the sauce over the servings.

Although the concentration of vitamins is greater in the green leaves, some people prefer the delicately cabbagelike flavor shepherd's purse takes on when blanched. Where, as so often happens, these edibles grow profusely near your home, you can experiment with blanching by anchoring paper bags over small groups of the young plants to exclude the sunlight.

The leaves, so bursting with vitamins but so low in calories, toughen as shepherd's purse matures. They then can be relegated to a small amount of boiling salted water, cooked until just tender, and dished out with the usual butter, margarine, vinegar, oil, hard-boiled egg, or other supplements.

Shepherd's purse, sometimes known as shepherd's heart and as pickpocket, is also used as a tea, 1 teaspoon to a cup of boiling water, 2 cups of which daily are said to stimulate sluggish kidneys. Too, pioneers sometimes soaked a handful of the leaves in water and used the latter to wash painful bruises.

MINER'S LETTUCE *(Montia)*

Stems and leaves of the well-known miner's lettuce—whose unmistakable feature is the way a pair of leaves grow together part way up some of the short stems and form a cup through whose middle the stalk continues—are estimable salad food when young and a better-than-average spinach substitute when older.

Miner's lettuce, also known as Indian lettuce and Spanish lettuce and in Europe as winter purslane, is one of the most abundant springtime edibles of the Pacific regions from British Columbia to Mexico, extending eastward to North Dakota. It grows from a dainty plant several inches high to a foot tall in moist shaded areas in woods, orchards, pastures, vineyards, fields, gardens, and along stream banks.

The succulent leaves differ considerably in shape, from the easily recognizable round leaves that encircle the tasty stems to form disks or cups to fleshy long-stemmed leaves that are sometimes triangular or even kidney-shaped. At the bottom, furthermore, clusters a spread of longish, more slender leaves through which several stems often arise. These are tougher than the others.

MINER'S LETTUCE

The plant is topped with small, edible, white or pinkish flowers that nod in loose bunches. These develop into shiny black seeds that furnish food for such upland game birds as dove and quail.

Hard-boiled eggs in particular bring out the subtle flavor of miner's lettuce, but these former objects should not be the leathery articles that are often served to unsuspecting diners. Instead, get enough water boiling in a pan to cover the eggs by 1 inch. Place the eggs in the pan with a spoon and let the temperature immediately drop to a simmer, keeping it that way until the eggs are done. Keep the eggs simmering, completely covered, for 8 to 10 minutes. Then remove from the heat and plunge into cold water. If the shells are cracked slightly before the eggs cool, peeling will be easier.

For a miner's lettuce salad for 2 hearty appetites, mix 4 cups of miner's lettuce, any stems chopped, with 2 chopped, hard-boiled eggs. Moisten liberally with 4 parts oil, preferably olive, and 1 part tarragon vinegar. Salt and pepper to taste, with freshly ground black pepper if you have it. Sit down to this at once, as the dressing will take the crispness out of the greens all too quickly.

When the Forty-Niners stampeded up California's streams and into its deserts and mountains in their search for gold, the lack of fresh food brought scurvy to some camps. It was the Indians and Spanish who helped some of these argonauts cure the vitamin-deficiency disease by introducing them to the succulencies of miner's lettuce. Those miners who didn't care for salad, or who gathered the edible so late in the season that it was tough, settled for boiling it, ideally briefly in a small amount of salted water.

WILD CELERY *(Angelica)*

Wild celery, also known as seacoast angelica, is even juicier and tastier than the celery you buy in stores. It grows in damp fields, beside moist roadsides, and along rocky or sandy coastlines from New England and eastern Canada to British Columbia and Alaska. It is at its best in late spring and early summer, while still tender.

The erect green stalks of this perennial, which are hollow, are coarse with many oil veins and often sticky patches. Growing up to about four feet tall, they are topped with numerous umbrellalike clusters of flowers, the individual members of which are small with five green or whitish petals. These eventually develop into small, angular, ribbed, dry fruits.

Wild celery is leafy, with the leaves growing in three thick groups of leaflets from stalks whose spreading bases sheathe the main stem. The roughly and unevenly toothed green leaflets, from one to three inches long, are thickly egg-shaped and have the odor of fresh celery.

Both the stems and leaf stalks are gathered when young, peeled, and their juicy interiors eaten with the same relish that is accorded the choicest celery. They are often boiled, too, sometimes in two changes of water if the user prefers a

WILD CELERY

more subdued taste. Wild celery also imparts a piquant flavor to boiled fish. You'll probably like it, too, in soup. Besides these ordinary ways of preparing wild celery, there are rather more complicated but delectable methods of bringing out the best of this succulent wild edible.

Creamed wild celery tastes like more. Melt ¼ cup butter or margarine, add ½ cup flour, and cook slowly for 5 minutes. Meanwhile heat 3 cups milk, not allowing it to boil. Pour this bit by bit into the flour mixture, stirring and cooking about 15 minutes until everything is smooth. Add ½ teaspoon salt, several shakes of pepper, and ½ cup grated cheese, which should be as snappy as you like it. Continue stirring as the cheese melts. The result may be poured over just boiled wild celery stalks and stems which have been peeled before cooking.

Braised wild celery is well worth the trouble, especially when you're famished from a windy afternoon along the shores. Peel the young stalks and stems, cut them into easily handled lengths, and halve them lengthwise. Lay them atop a base of thinly sliced onions in a shallow pan, cover with warm water in which 2 chicken or beef bouillon cubes have been dissolved, and simmer in the oven for about 15 minutes, or until very tender.

In the meantime, gently sauté some finely chopped onion with a generous amount of butter or margarine in a frypan until it has reached a golden brown. Soften the taste with a little red wine if you want. Then remove the wild celery to a baking dish. Pour the sauce over it. Sprinkle liberally with Parmesan cheese and return to the oven for baking until the cheese has melted.

SCOTCH LOVAGE *(Ligusticum)*

Scotch or sea lovage, another of the wild celeries, grows in wind-swept sandy and gravelly stretches along northern seacoasts from New York to Alaska. It has long been a favorite green and cooked vegetable among the coast-dwelling Scots, who early discovered it here during their excursions to the New World. Rich in vitamins A and C, it is particularly tasty with fish. It also can be made into a better than passable confection.

Although its leaves and flowers resemble those of the previously described wild celery *(Angelica)*, Scotch lovage grows more like domestic celery in that its long-stalked leaves rise directly from the base of the perennial instead of growing from a main stem. Each of these leafy stalks, which clasp the plant with broadly sheathlike bases that are reddish or purplish, ends in three oval, roughly toothed, shiny leaflets from one to three inches long.

SCOTCH LOVAGE

The white or pinkish flowers grow in flattish, umbrella-like clusters on the ends of thin stems up to about two and one-half feet high. They produce short, tan, dryish, oblong fruits. The roots are stout and deep.

The fresh young stalks and leaves are best before the plant blossoms. Although I do not find Scotch lovage's flavor resembling celery's as closely as does the wild celery of the *Angelica* family, it can be used interchangeably, either raw or cooked, in the recipes suggested for the former vegetables. One often finds stalks that have been blanched by being partially covered with wind-driven debris, and these have a blander flavor that many people enjoy more in salads and hors d'oeuvres.

Scotch lovage goes well with hard-boiled eggs. This recipe takes a little work but is worthwhile, especially if you are having company and want to make a special effort.

Halve the eggs, which have been simmered in a covered pan for 10 minutes and then plunged into cold water to ease the peeling. Remove the yolks, which, cooked this way, should be firm and mealy. Mash them and add 2 tablespoons mayonnaise, a few sprinkles of vinegar, and salt and pepper to taste. Mix in an equal bulk of tender young Scotch lovage and sweet pickles, chopped up in equal amounts. Refill the halved whites.

Scotch lovage will also provide a unique and spicy candy. Boil conveniently short sections of root or young stalks until a fork penetrates them easily. Then simmer, covered, for 15 minutes in a syrup made in the proportions of 1 cup of sugar to each cup of water. Although it isn't necessary, you can, if you want, give added crunchiness to the finished products by rolling them in granulated sugar before laying them aside to cool and dry.

MOUNTAIN SORREL (*Oxyria*)

Mountain sorrel is a green we've enjoyed in such diverse places as New Mexico, British Columbia, and the green-sloped White Mountains of New Hampshire. This member of the buckwheat family, which grows from Alaska and Greenland to Southern California, is also widely enjoyed in Europe and Asia. It is known in different parts of this country as sourgrass, scurvy grass, and Alpine sorrel.

The perennial mountain sorrel springs from a few inches to two feet high from a large, thick, deep, fleshy root. The small leaves, growing one or two on stems that for the most part rise directly from the rootstock, are smooth and either round or broadly kidney-shaped. Scarcely noticeable greenish or crimson flowers grow in rising clusters on long, full stems that extend above the mostly basal leaves. These blossoms turn into tiny reddish capsules.

MOUNTAIN SORREL

The juicy leaves, which are at their best before the plant flowers, have a pleasantly acid taste which somewhat resembles that of rhubarb. In fact, mountain sorrel looks to some like miniature rhubarb, although it so happens that the leaves of domestic rhubarb, whether raw or cooked, are poisonous. Those of mountain sorrel, on the other hand, are delicious for salads, potherbs, and purees. Where this wild edible grows in the Arctic, Eskimos both in America and

Asia ferment some of it as a sauerkraut. The tender young leaves will also give a zip to sandwiches.

Mountain sorrel leaves can be turned into a puree by simmering them for 20 minutes, then pressing them through a colander or mashing them, and adding butter or margarine, salt, and pepper. You'll save vitamins, flavor, and time, though, if you use a meat grinder or kitchen blender on these juicy greens, then quickly cook and add them to a piping hot base.

For a memorable cream soup, pour a quart of rich milk into a pan and set over low heat. When it starts to bubble, add 3 cups of mountain sorrel puree and salt and pepper to taste. Simmer for 5 minutes, stirring. Then gradually pour 3 beaten egg yolks into the mixture, stirring energetically until the color is even. Remove from the heat and, using a fork, blend in 4 tablespoons of butter or margarine. Serve immediately.

You can capitalize on the excellent way mountain sorrel combines with the delicate flavor of fish by making a thick fish stock, slowly bringing the heads, tails, bones, fins, and even the scales, if any, to a boil in cold water to cover, and simmering all afternoon along with a chopped onion and, if you want, a kernel of garlic. You'll need about 1/3 pound of such remnants for each individual, so wait until the fishing has been good.

Just before you're ready to sit down to the table, heat in proportional amounts for each diner 1 cup strained fish stock, ¼ teaspoon salt, and a sprinkling of black pepper. Stir in an equal amount of mountain sorrel puree, simmer for 5 minutes, and serve hot with a liberal pat of butter or margarine spreading atop.

Mountain sorrel adds a pungency to green salads, especially when about one-fourth as much water cress is added to contrast with its flavorsome sourness. We usually prefer a plain oil dressing, carefully touched up with a very little salt to taste. It's doubtful if you'll want any vinegar. Such salads go especially well with fish, crabs, and lobsters.

Boiled, mountain sorrel combines well with other greens, its acidity giving them added flavor. Because of this acidness, it is best to season gradually to taste and, in most cases, to omit the usual vinegar or lemon juice. A complement of hard-boiled eggs and crisp bacon, both thinly sliced, goes well with these greens.

Always welcome is this robust soup, individually seasoned. For 4 fishermen, the procedure is to start it by dicing about ½ pound bacon and, starting with a cold frypan, slowly bringing this to a sputter. Let the bits become crisp by tilting the pan so that the grease will run to one side. Then spoon them temporarily onto a plate.

Have 8 medium-sized potatoes, 2 onions, and 4 cups of mountain sorrel leaves chopped and mixed. Add these to the bacon fat and stir occasionally until the potatoes start to tan. Then return the bacon, flatten out everything in the pan, cover with water, stir, and simmer until a fork penetrates the potatoes easily. By this time none of us has ever been able to wait any longer.

PASTURE BRAKE (*Pteridium*)

When I attended college in Maine, we used to see fiddleheads regularly displayed for sale in the spring in the Lewiston markets. Later, I used to feast on them while spring bear hunting in New Brunswick. We have relished them many times, more recently, in the West and Far North. They are the young, uncoiled fronds of the fern family's brakes, so called because in this emerging state they resemble the tuning ends of violins. They are also known in many localities as croziers because of their resemblance to the shepherds' crooklike staffs of bishops, abbots, and abbesses.

Although some other similar fronds are edible, it is the

fiddleheads from the widely familiar and distributed pasture brake, *Pteridium aquilinum,* that are most commonly enjoyed. These grow, often luxuriantly, through the Northern Hemisphere, in Europe and Asia as well as in North America. They are found, sometimes in waving acres that brush your knees as you ride through on horseback, from Alaska across Canada to Newfoundland, south through the states to California and Mexico.

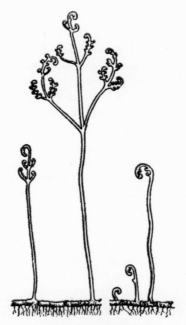

PASTURE BRAKE

These are edible, however, only while still fiddleheads and therefore young. They are then good both raw and cooked. Later, the full-grown fronds toughen and become poisonous to cattle as well as humans. While still in the uncurled state, on the other hand, they are found very acceptable by some of the wildlife, including the mountain beaver.

Pasture brake is known to different people as just plain brake, bracken, hog brake, bracken fern, eagle fern, brake fern, and Western bracken. It decorates often shady roadsides, dry open woods, pastures, clearings, and may often be seen adding welcome green to recently burned forests.

It is a coarse, perennial fern with a blackish root, so favored by the Japanese for thickening and flavoring soups that laws had to be passed there to prevent its extinction. Early in the spring, these roots send up scattered fiddleheads. These later uncoil and stretch into long, erect stalks with typically fernlike leaflets, whose greenness takes on a straw to purplish-brown color with maturity. The widely triangular fronds, which may be from one to three feet across, are distinctively separated into three usually broadly spreading branches.

The fiddleheads, too, are noticeably three-forked. They are easily recognized, also, because of the fact that they are often found near the tangled previous year's bracken, perhaps flattened by snows. They are best when not more than five to eight inches high, while still rusty with a woolly coating. Break them off with the fingers as low as they will snap easily, remove the loose brown coatings by rubbing them between the hands, and they're ready for eating. If you like vegetables which, like okra, are mucilaginous, you'll probably enjoy a few of these raw.

The rather pleasant ropy consistency of this delicately glutinous juice is changed to a certain extent by cooking, but the sweetish fiddleheads are still reminiscent of okra. One way to enjoy fiddleheads is simmered in a little salted water until tender, then salted and peppered to taste, and eaten hot with plenty of melting butter or margarine.

Or bedeck them with a mayonnaise, perhaps homemade. You can very satisfactorily prepare this in a soup plate, if you don't happen to have a flat-bottomed bowl, by dropping in 2 egg yolks and stirring them vigorously with a fork. Then add a cup of oil, preferably olive, although any good cooking oil will do, pouring it in bit by bit and continually mixing with a fork until both ingredients, thoroughly mixed, stiffen. Blend in a tablespoon of good wine vinegar, then salt and pepper to taste. Spoon liberally over the hot fiddleheads.

A supper of fiddleheads on hot buttered toast sets just right for people who don't feel like eating much. When served this way, the little wild vegetables retain more of their delicate flavor when steamed. After they are cleaned and washed, drop them into 2 tablespoons boiling water in the top of a double boiler. Cover the utensil, place over boiling water, and cook for 30 minutes. The best way to keep on retaining the distinctive flavor is just to salt each serving lightly to individual taste, then top with a generous slab of butter or margarine.

Tender young fiddleheads can also add a lot to a mixed green salad. Oil seems to bring out the taste more in these, and we like it mixed 4 to 1 with preferably a wine vinegar, although lemon juice is good, too.

In cold regions such as Alaska, fiddleheads are often canned for opening as a winter vegetable. They delectably thicken soups. It may be well to remember, too, in case of a possible emergency, that the long rootstocks can be roasted, peeled, and, if you want, powdered Indian fashion, after which the nourishingly starchy insides may either be eaten as is or used as flour.

DOCK *(Rumex)*

The more than a dozen docks thriving on this continent from the Arctic coast of Alaska southward throughout the United States provide hearty greens which were widely eaten by the Indians, some tribes of which used the abundant seeds in grinding meal. The Eskimos still put up quantities for winter use. This wild edible, also eaten in Europe and Asia, has a more rugged flavor than some of the other wild vegetables. Having overtones of both sourness and bitterness that

DOCK
Top: leaves; *Bottom:* stalk with flowers.

vary with the different species, it is often preferred mixed with other greens.

The docks as a whole have certain distinctive characteristics that are easy to identify. Furthermore, they are well known as edibles in many areas, sometimes as wild spinach, and are even cultivated in some regions. They are often troublesome in cultivated fields, pastures, vacant lots, alongside roads, and with provoking frequency in lawns.

Docks are stoutish plants, bearing their leaves sometimes two feet long or occasionally heart-shaped, with smooth undersides, mostly around their bases. Where the fleshy leafstalks are attached to the stem, papery membranous sheaths wrap themselves around the joints.

The numerous tiny flowers, greenish or tinted with purple, crowd together on insignificant stems on long batonlike stalks up to about five feet tall. The erect dry stalks can be seen in the fall, rusty with multitudinous seeds that are ready to be scattered on thin, ribbed wings by the wind.

If dock is picked young enough, it makes a better than average salad, although I prefer to add it to such other greens as dandelion, mustard, and water cress, when these are available. Because of its somewhat lemonish flavor, you may prefer to skip the vinegar, using oil, salt, and pepper alone.

Dock to me is best rapidly boiled in a small amount of salted water only until tender, then served at once with butter or margarine. It does usually gain a certain amount of bitterness with age, however, and people who object to this should change the boiling water once or twice. However, the less these green leaves are cooked, the richer they are in vitamins and minerals.

The delicately bitter, lemonlike flavor of dock makes a lot of seasoning unnecessary, although, like other wild greens, it is often cooked with ham, bacon, or salt pork. However, steamed with something as mild as butter, dock is excellent.

Some docks lose considerably more bulk in cooking than others, but depending on what you're using, you'll need about 6 cups of shredded dock, washed and drained, for 2 liberal servings. Melt 2 level tablespoons butter in a large, preferably heavy frypan over high heat. Stir in the dock, add 2 tablespoons of water, and cover. Stirring occasionally, cook for 2 or 3 minutes, or until the greens are wilted. Sprinkle with salt and serve.

You can also capitalize on the way dock's unique flavor blends with sea food by making a steaming clam soup. Brown 1 large chopped onion only until softly tan, not black, in 4 tablespoons butter or margarine. Then scatter in 2 cups finely shredded young dock leaves and stir for about a minute until they wilt. Add 2 cups cleaned clams, either fresh or canned, and 2 cups rich milk. Bring to a slow simmer for not more than a minute, as cooking toughens clams. Dust with pepper. You probably won't want any salt. For 2 persons, there should be enough for seconds.

COMMON CHICKWEED *(Stellaria)* *(Alsine)*

You can find this meek little member of the pink family blooming almost everywhere in the central United States every month, although its deeply notched white flowers open only in sunshine. It grows in fields, gardens, waste lands, cultivated grounds, woods, and in moist places generally throughout this country and most of the world.

Easily recognized and therefore a good emergency food for stranded and hungry people, this annual is unique in that it begins growing in the fall, survives the severities of cold even in the North, starts blossoming in late winter, and often finishes its life cycle and valuable seed production in the springtime. These numberless tiny seeds in their papery capsules, and the plant's tender leaves, are enjoyed by many game birds. Mountain sheep also eat them.

Botanists have different ideas about this family, not only as to its name, *Stellaria* or *Alsine*, but also as to the number of immediate relations. There may be as many as some seventy-five different species according to some counts, about twenty-five of which grow in this country. Only one of these, however, is important as a human and wildlife food.

COMMON CHICKWEED

Common chickweed is a low, sprawling plant with weak and brittle stems up to about a foot long. Leaves grow in opposite pairs on numerous slender branches. These leaves, which are smoothly oval and rather sharply pointed, are attached directly to the upper parts of the branches but grow from hairy stems along their lower portions.

The small white flowers, clustering at the leafy ends of the branches or stemming from where other leaves meet the branches, have five petals that are so deeply cleft that at first glance they may seem to be ten narrow ones. These develop into papery capsules that are filled with tiny seeds that some people gather for their appreciative canaries.

There's nothing fancy about common chickweed, but it is an abundant green that boils up wholesomely in a little salted water and, topped with an extra amount of butter or margarine, has none of the disagreeable taste that many people find in spinach. If only the top stems and leaves are used, these will become tender in a very short time. Use vinegar, chopped bacon, or both to pep up the delicate taste when guests find it a little too bland. Or, when you can, mix common chickweed half and half with dandelions, mustard, or water cress.

Besides eating this plant, pioneers used to crush the fresh leaves and use them as poultices, replacing them once or twice daily. An ointment was made also by bruising new leaves in fresh lard and using this as a cooling application for skin irritation.

WINTER CRESS *(Barbarea)*

The yellow mustardlike flowers of the winter cress—also known as yellow rocket, Belle Island cress, scurvy grass, bitter cress, spring cress, and upland cress—are familiar sights in fields, gardens, meadows, pastures, and along roadsides, especially in the East where three of this country's four species occur. There are two closely related, look-alike cousins, *Barbarea verna* and *Barbarea vulgaris,* which share the same seasons, are equally good to eat, and are often seen growing together.

The clusters of small four-petaled golden blossoms, resembling tiny Maltese crosses, show that these edible herbs belong among the numerous species of native and European mustards. As a matter of fact, winter cress is cultivated both here and abroad both as a winter salad green and as a potherb.

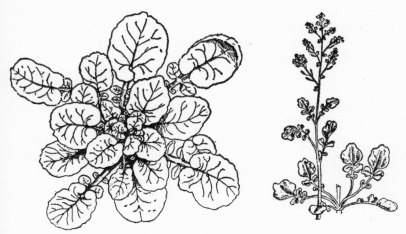

WINTER CRESS
Left: mature rosette; *Right:* early rosette and stalk with flowers.

These sunny little flowers, growing in groups between the upper leaves and the stalks, and at the tops of the angled stems, evolve into narrow, rather acutely four-angled pods up to three inches long. The smooth stems, usually growing one to two feet high, become thick with long, glossy, green leaves that have none of the hairiness of some of the other mustards.

The main importance of winter cress lies in its unusual aptitude for growing robustly during mild winter weather where the ground is clear of snow. In fact, its Latin name *Barbarea* recognizes that new young leaves and stems are often ready for the table on St. Barbara's Day which arrives every December 4. Actually, if the initial rosettes of long, dark green, smooth leaves are not gathered when they first spread directly from the perennial and biennial roots during winter and early spring, they become overly bitter. Besides, this early seasonableness of winter cress gives you an additional reason to enjoy balmy winter periods out of doors.

This first of the year's greens in many localities gives character to mixed salads and, when freshly gathered, is far richer in healthful vitamins than any of the artificially fertilized, sprayed, and much handled greens you can buy in the store. Try it, too, in a smothered salad.

Just before you are ready to eat, shred enough young leaves to provide 3 cupfuls. Chop 3 young green onions, including the tops, into fine pieces and mix thoroughly with the winter cress. Add 1 teaspoon sugar and salt to taste. Pour 2 tablespoons vinegar over everything.

In the meantime, cut 6 slices of bacon into thin strips, put in a cold frypan, and fry slowly until crisp, tilting the pan so that the grease will run away from the meat. Then add the bacon to the salad and pour the hot drippings over it. Toss and serve while everything is fresh and crisp.

Winter cress also provides estimable boiling greens. During the cold seasons while still young, it is no more bitter than some lettuce. Later, though, you may prefer to simmer it in 2 waters, pouring out the first. Early in the season I prefer it with just butter or margarine melting on top, but a little later on vinegar seems to bring out the somewhat radishlike flavor better.

It's true that the leaves take on too much bitterness for enjoyable eating when winter cress finally blooms, but then the buds have a broccolilike savoriness. These grow in clusters at the tops of the flowering stalks, making for quick and easy gathering. As with dandelions, the inclusion of a few open flowers does not hurt the taste. However, if you'd prefer to make the flavor a little more subtle, first pour boiling water over the harvest and allow it to stand a minute before draining.

Then, in any event, immerse the buds in a small amount of boiling water, simmer for about 4 minutes, and then drain at once. Be sure not to overcook, or the buds will become mushy. We like these topped with just a melting daub of butter or margarine. They are good with a few dashes of vinegar and a frosting of finely chopped onion, too.

FIREWEED (*Epilobium*) (*Chamaenerion*)

Fireweed, which in summer gives an unforgettable amethyst hue to vast fire-blackened stretches below some of my favorite sheep and goat ranges west of the Alaska Highway, is another wild vegetable difficult to mistake. Thousands of square miles of burned lands from the Aleutians and Greenland to Mexico soften to magenta annually, so showily do these tall perennials flame into spikelike clusters of flowers.

Two species of fireweed enhance most of the northern wooded sections of the continent from the Far North south to California, Kansas, and the Carolinas. These gaunt, pink-to-purple-flowered members of the evening primrose family spring up in otherwise unsightly areas bared by logging operations, forest fires, and road clearings, stretching skywards from one to eight feet.

The showy flowers, which grow loosely in terminal spikes, begin blossoming at the bottom of the single stem and slowly climb upward. The lance-shaped leaves resemble those of the willow. As the warm weather proceeds, the flowers evolve into small pods which later become shaggy with white-tufted seeds that fill air and streams in the fall.

Fireweeds, with their profusion of small magenta blossoms, are valuable honey flowers, and beekeepers sometimes move their hives to the vicinity of recent logging operations to capitalize on them. Around our log cabin in northern British Columbia, I have often seen moose browsing on the plants. Deer eat them, too.

Try cutting the young stems into sections and boiling them in a small amount of salted water until tender. This way they resemble asparagus. In fact, where I was hunting on the Gaspé Peninsula in Quebec one time, the local French Canadians called this wild edible *asperge*—wild asparagus.

FIREWEED

More mature stalks can be peeled and their sweetish interiors either eaten raw or cooked into thick soup. Young fireweed leaves cook up into satisfactory greens. But even if you can't get to these until fall, all is not lost. Steep them for tea.

Young fireweed is good on occasion pan-steamed with butter. These plants grow so abundantly that you shouldn't have any trouble in picking a quantity of the small, tender leaves. For 2 diners, measure 4 loose cups of these. Then melt 2 tablespoons butter or margarine in a large, preferably heavy frypan over high heat. Stir in the greens and 3 table-spoons of water. Cover and, stirring periodically, cook about 2 minutes, or until the fireweed is wilted. Salt and pepper to taste. Eat while still hot and savory.

WILLOW (*Salix*)

This favorite browse of deer, elk, and moose is included here because, being so widely distributed and so easily identified, it is a food that in an emergency could save your life.

Between 200 and 300 varieties of willow grow in the world, about one-third of them thriving all over this country. They prefer damp fertile bottomlands, stream edges which they often hold in place, and lake and pond rims, but some are also seen in high, rocky country. They vary from big graceful trees to tiny shoots and shrubs, only a few inches high, in arctic and alpine regions.

Often the first spring source of Vitamin C, the buds and sprouts of these latter species provide the main subsistence of ptarmigan. Several species of grouse look to willow buds and tender portions of the twigs for food, while rabbits and many of the hoofed browsers seek twigs, foliage, and bark for nourishment.

It is not hard for the average individual to distinguish a willow from other trees and shrubs, especially when varieties become downy with the well-known pussy willows. The willows have alternate, or very occasionally opposite, leaves with smooth or toothed margins. Most species have long and narrow, or oblong lance-shaped leaves with short stems.

The twigs are slim, round, pliable, and often brittle at the base. The buds, usually very flat on the side next to the twig while bulging roundly on the outer side, are covered with a solitary scale apiece. The majority of the willows are shrubby. The bark of many species is bitter with salicin, used in medicine as a tonic and to reduce fever.

WILLOW
Left: branch with leaves; *Right:* winter twigs.

Young willow shoots can be gathered at the beginning of warm weather, peeled of their outer bark, and their tender insides eaten raw. The tender young leaves, some of which have been found to be up to ten times richer in Vitamin C than oranges, are also edible raw.

So is the thin layer of inner bark which, after the outside bark has been removed, can be scraped free with a knife. This is tastiest at the start of the growing season. Bitterish in many species of willow, in others it is surprisingly sweet. Too, this inner bark is sometimes dried and ground into flour.

WILD RICE (*Zizania*)

The two native varieties of wild rice, which are tagged with probably surprisingly high prices in the corner market but which flavorwise are worth nearly every penny of it, grow free for the eating throughout much of the East from southern Canada to the Gulf of Mexico. This notable Indian food reaches its most opulent abundance in the north country from Maine and New Brunswick to the eastern reaches of the prairies and in lush fresh water marshes along the Atlantic seaboard. It has also been widely transplanted as a duck food, often successfully where soft, deep mud and gently circulating water are present.

This coarsely large, plume-topped grass grows luxuriantly on mucky or silty bottoms in shallow water where there is enough circulation to prevent stagnation. Black ducks, canvasbacks, mallards, pintails, redheads, wood ducks, and snow geese are among the waterfowl who seek it out in swamps and marshes, and often where it grows in great stands along the rivers, lakes, and ponds that are favorites of sportsmen.

Growing from four to ten feet tall, with a stout stem nearly half an inch through at the bottom, it will hardly be mistaken for anything else. The leaves are long and narrow, averaging between one and three feet long and close to an inch wide. The plants are tipped with long clusters of flowers that are of two different kinds, pollen-bearing below and seed-bearing toward the top. The slender seeds become dark and rodlike, expanding in husks that are stiffly tipped with a hairlike growth.

These husks are loose, however, and not difficult to remove. The secret is to spread the rice in a warm shelter, perhaps on newspapers in the attic, until it is dry. Then parch it in a moderately warm oven for three hours, reaching in a hand and mixing it occasionally, so it will dry evenly without burning. The husks can then be freed by beating or, if you have only a small amount, by rubbing the seeds between the palms. The easiest way I know of to blow away the chaff is by pouring the rice back and forth between two receptacles in a good breeze. Store in a dry place in well-closed containers.

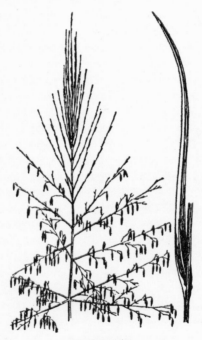

WILD RICE
Left: stalk; *Right:* leaf and stem.

A more important consideration is harvesting the crop during the latter half of summer or in early autumn when, depending on the local climate, it will be ripe and waiting. The mature seeds soon fall from the plants, but on the other hand they adhere too tenaciously for easy gathering while still green. The Indian way of getting in wild rice is still a good one. This consists of spreading a large canvas over the bottom of a canoe, paddling among the plants, bending the stalks over the canoe, and beating the seeds out on the tarpaulin with a stick.

The only drawback to this delicacy, unless you harvest it yourself for free, is the expense of the purple-black seeds with their smoky sweetness, so excellent with game and poultry. Incidentally, if wild rice is not well washed in cold water before using, it will have too much of this smoky flavor.

Although it is too precious to be used indiscriminately, wild rice will improve any recipe I know of calling for the domestic grain. To start off with, why not just stir 1 cup of the wild product into 1½ cups boiling water, seasoned with a teaspoon of salt. Do this so slowly that the bubbling does not stop. Cover and simmer without stirring for about 30 minutes, or until you can bite smoothly through a test kernel. If you're not pressed for time, put the rice in a sieve and set this in the emptied pot over the heat to dry in the rising hot air. Enjoy the different taste hot with butter, cream, or both.

Then maybe you'd like to try some wild rice croquettes, particularly if there is some game to serve them with. Cook a cup of rice with 1½ cups of already bubbling chicken or similar broth in a double boiler for 50 minutes, or until fluffy. Then put in a pan with 3 tablespoons white bread crumbs, 1 beaten egg, 4 tablespoons melted butter or margarine, and salt and pepper to taste. Mix well and then shape into small balls. Roll these in 3 tablespoons flour, then in a whipped egg, and finally in 4 tablespoons of bread crumbs. Fry in deep, hot fat for 2 or 3 minutes until golden brown. Eat at once.

Fried wild rice can be good, too. Start by boiling 1 cup of the smoky seeds until tender. In the meantime, melt ½ pound butter or margarine in a large frypan. Add 2 small chopped onions, a cup of minced ham or other cooked meat, and a minced clove of garlic. Then add the strained rice, salt and pepper to taste, and sauté another 5 minutes, stirring constantly.

You can even have popped wild rice. Place a small quantity of your best, newly gathered, still unwashed seeds in a fine sieve. Immerse this in deep hot fat until the kernels pop. Drain on paper towels, salt, and serve. This goes particularly well evenings with some of the cool wild fruit juices.

Wild Roots And Tubers

Instead of potatoes, carrots, parsnips, radishes, beets, and turnips as we now know them, Indians often relied on wild roots and tubers, especially in those parts of the arid West where the lack of rainfall made gardening nearly impossible. When pioneers, prospectors, and others later began daring the plains and deserts, many of them starved amidst abundance, because they didn't know what to eat or how to prepare it.

The tuberous roots of the arrowhead, sometimes stumbled over by starving men where it grows in marshy ground, were relished by a number of tribes. Jerusalem artichokes, distinctively flavored tubers of a native wild sunflower long cultivated by the Indians, became so popular among early settlers that they were introduced into Europe. During colonial days, too, the still widely used sassafras roots became in great demand in England and on the European continent.

Many of the first settlers in Virginia became fond, through necessity, of the sweetish young roots of the cattail. The venturesome Swedes who early brought their log cabins to the Delaware River depended on groundnuts because of the lack of bread.

GROUNDNUT *(Apios)*

The Pilgrims, shown the groundnut by friendly Indians, relied on them to a large extent their first rugged winter in Plymouth. Other Indians along the eastern seaboard regularly ate these potatolike vegetables. They thus became known to early white settlers, many of whom found them very acceptable substitutes for bread. Today they can provide interesting supplements to the most modern of meals, while in an emergency they can still prevent starving.

The perennial vines of this member of the pea family twine across low damp places and along the edges of swamps and streams, climbing where they can. They are found from New Brunswick to Florida and the Gulf of Mexico, west to Ontario, Kansas, and Texas. Growing up in New England where the groundnut is still comparatively well known, I was introduced to it early. Other names include Indian potato, bog potato, and wild bean.

You can smell the memorable sweetness of the flowering vine well before you reach it. The abundant brownish or purplish flowers, growing late in the summer in thick clusters from the junctures of the leaves and the soft vines, resemble those of garden beans and peas. The small, slender pods, in turn, look like those of garden beans. When you can collect enough of them, the seeds inside may be prepared like peas. Alternate leaves, each with five to nine egg-shaped leaflets from one to three inches long growing from its stalk on very short stems, angle out from the vines, which have a milky sap.

GROUNDNUT

The groundnuts grow in a chain of tuberlike enlargements, sometimes as big as eggs, on the long roots. Lying in strings just beneath the surface, these can be easily uncovered by hand unless the ground is frozen.

Edible raw, groundnuts are better cooked. Incidentally, their taste either way has more overtones of turnips than of potatoes. To cook them, just drop them into salted boiling water, simmer them until a fork passes through them easily, and then eat them unpeeled with melting butter or margarine. If any are left over, slice and fry these, as they lack both taste and tenderness when cold.

ARROWHEAD *(Sagittaria)*

Indians from the Pacific to the Atlantic ate the potatolike roots of the arrowhead, usually either boiling them or roasting them in the hot ashes of campfires. Related species are also enjoyed in Europe, and in Asia, where some Chinese cultivate them along the damp rims of rice paddies. In fact, when numerous Chinese moved into California, where this common wild plant is known as the tule potato, they quickly adopted it, and it is sometimes seen in the nearby markets.

In other words, the arrowhead is one of the most valuable native food plants and, nutritious and delectable, is well worth eating. Today, however, it is mostly idly observed by fishermen whipping their lines along the edges of ponds and sluggish streams from the southern half of Canada, throughout most of the United States, to deep into Mexico. Starving men, too, sometimes stumble over it where it grows in fresh, marshy ground.

There are some twenty or more species of *Sagittaria,* all bearing edible tubers, scattered in wet, non-saline places throughout the continent. About seven of these have large starchy bulbs. The differences in the plants are usually minor, and there is no need to try to separate them. Other names include arrowleaf, duck potato, and swan potato, as well as the Indian cognomens of wapatoo and katniss. Ducks, geese, and muskrats feast on the tubers when they are not too large nor buried too deeply. Ducks also eat the small flattish seeds.

Despite the name, all the leaves of this five- to thirty-six-inch-tall member of the water plantain family are not arrow-shaped. Growing from four to twelve inches long atop clusters of long erect stems, which thrust up directly from the fibrous roots, these are sometimes long and uniform in width and occasionally lance-shaped.

ARROWHEAD
Top: stalks, leaves, and flowers; *Bottom:* tuber.

The white flowers, blooming from July to September, are readily recognized. Fragile and three-petaled, they usually appear in groups near the top of a naked spire that sometimes extends one or two feet above the leaves. The golden-centered, uppermost blossoms are male. Lower down, green-cored female flowers await fertilization pollen from other plants. Rounded heads of flat, winged seeds are later produced.

The hard little tubers, looking much like potatoes and varying from the most used size of eggs to that of BB shot, grow at the ends of often long subterranean runners, sometimes a few feet beyond the plant. Mature after midsummer and in the fall, they are also toothsome throughout the winter.

During these seasons, wading Indians used their toes to dislodge the bulbs, which then readily floated when freed of root and mud. However, you can generally find these native perennials growing thickly along the muddy edges of nearby swamps and shallow ponds where, perhaps wearing boots, you can speedily and repeatedly dig all you can use with a vigorously wielded hoe.

Arrowhead tubers can be eaten raw in an emergency, but they taste better cooked. They can be enjoyed baked, boiled, creamed, roasted, French-fried, and scalloped just like new potatoes, which, in our opinion, they excel, having a unique smoothness and sweetness. They require more cooking than white potatoes of the same size, and they are the better for peeling afterward.

Our favorite arrowhead repast, which we usually enjoy several times every fall, is a cooked salad. For use as a hearty main dish for 2 people, scrub and boil 5 heaping cups of the tubers, removing them from the salted water after 25 minutes while they are a little hard. Peel as sparingly as possible so as to preserve the utmost flavor and nourishment. Hard-boil 6 eggs at the same time; then plunge them under cold water and peel them.

Slice some of the hot arrowhead into a large bowl. Slice some eggs atop it. Now pour on a liberal amount of olive oil or salad oil. Douse on about ¼ as much vinegar. Salt and pepper. Sprinkle on a very small amount of powdered garlic, if desired. Paprika and dried parsley will add eye and taste appeal. Repeat until you've used all the tubers and eggs. Cover so that the flavor will permeate everything.

Preparing this salad half a day or more ahead of time will give the best results. Take off the lid once or twice and carefully, so as not to break up the eggs and tubers, spoon the mixture around a bit to redistribute the oil and vinegar. The superbly harmonizing taste of arrowhead always manages to give this treat that special something.

CHICORY (*Cichorium*)

Chicory, millions of pounds of whose roots have been used as an adulterant and as a substitute for coffee, also provides greens for salads and for cooking whose excellence gives them prime positions on the vegetable counters of many local markets. Long popular in Europe, too, chicory is an escapee from that continent and from Asia. It now grows throughout most of the United States and across Canada from British Columbia to Nova Scotia.

Resembling the dandelion both in appearance and taste, it has, however, usually bright blue flowers which, except in cloudy weather when they may stay open all day, generally open only in the morning sunshine and shut by noon. These beautiful wheel-like blossoms, which sometimes spread like soft blue mist along roadsides and across grassy pastures and fields, also give the plant its other common name of blue sailor. It is also known as succory.

This rigid perennial with its angular branches grows from a long, deep taproot and reaches a height of from one to five feet. As in the familiar dandelion, the leaves nearly all grow at the bottom of the plant, starting underground and spreading in a rosette just above the surface. They are narrowly long and coarsely lobed or toothed. Smaller, clasping leaves ascend the stem. The flowers, which often grace the landscape from July to October, are occasionally whitish or pink and are made up of at least two uneven ranks of strap-shaped petals whose ends are toothed. Chicory's sap is bitter and milky.

We use the basal chicory leaves just as we do those of the similar dandelion, although when gathering them in the

CHICORY
Top: branch with flowers; *Bottom:* rosette.

early spring, we take pains to dig deeply enough to uncover the delicate white portions that grow underground directly from the deep root. You can also upend paper bags over groups of plants and bleach the entire lengths of the leaves. Although only pleasantly bitter at first and hard to equal for salads, maturing and toughening chicory leaves all too soon become excessively bitter even when boiled in several changes of salted water. So get them well before they flower.

Much of the chicory root used in this country as a coffee substitute, stretcher, and flavorer, is imported from Europe, but exactly the same thing grows right here at home. If you'd like to make your own, just dig some of the long roots, scrub them with a brush, and then roast them slowly in a partly open oven until they will break crisply between the fingers, exposing a dark brown interior. Then grind and store in a closed container for brewing as a coffee substitute, in lesser amounts, as it's stronger, or for blending with your regular supply of the bean.

JERUSALEM ARTICHOKE *(Helianthus)*

Jerusalem artichokes, distinctively flavored tubers of a native wild sunflower, were cultivated by Indians and much used by early settlers. Besides still growing wild, they are also raised for today's markets, all of which indicates how well worth finding they are.

They have no connection with the Holy City. Soon introduced into Europe following Columbus' voyages to the New World, they became popular along the Mediterranean and were called *girasole* in Italian and *girasol* in Spanish. These words, denoting sunflower, became corrupted in English to *Jerusalem*. The artichoke part of the name stems from the fact that even centuries ago the flower buds of some of the edible sunflowers were boiled and eaten with butter like that vegetable.

About ninety species of sunflowers occur in the world. Some two-thirds of these grow in the United States, among them these tall perennials whose roots are such a delicacy. You have to like them, of course. We've learned to prepare them so that we do.

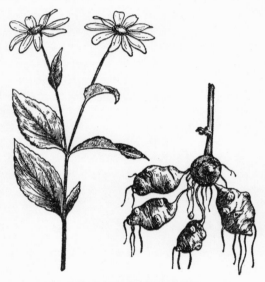

JERUSALEM ARTICHOKE
Left: stalk with leaves and flowers; *Right:* tubers.

Wild Jerusalem artichokes, which should be harvested no sooner than fall, are native to the central parts of the United States and Canada. Their popularity among Indians and arriving Europeans, plus their cultivation in different parts of the country, helps explain why this native has long since escaped its original bounds and is now often found in abundance elsewhere—such as east of the Appalachians, where it has moved to usually moist soil along ditches, streams, roadways, fence rows, and in vacant fields and lots.

These perennial sunflowers grow with thin stalks commonly five to ten feet tall. The rough leaves, whose tops are hairy, develop sharp points from oblong or egg-shaped bodies that are broadest near their bases. The frequently numerous flowers are yellow. From two to three inches broad, and maturing on slender stems that rise from where the higher leaves meet the stalk, these blossoms lack the purplish and brownish centers of those sunflowers that yield edible, oil-rich seeds. But the tubers, which are attached to the thickly creeping roots, more than make up for this deficiency.

History is all in favor of these delicacies whose somewhat sweetish juiciness, however, may take a bit of getting accustomed to. On the other hand, Jerusalem artichokes are nutritious and easily digestible enough to be regarded as a favored food for invalids. Here are a couple of hints that may help along your enjoyment. Dig them late in the year, even in winter if the ground is not too frozen, previously noting their whereabouts when they are conspicuously in bloom. Secondly, take care that they are not cooked too long nor at too high temperatures, as both toughen them.

Your cooking efforts may be as simple or as elaborate as you want them to be. The long, somewhat flat tubers are good just scrubbed, simmered in their skins in enough water to cover until just tender, and then peeled and served like potatoes, either with salt and butter or margarine or with a cream sauce. They then afford a by-product, too. When cold, the water in which they were boiled becomes jellylike, providing a flavorful and substantial foundation for soup.

Or, if you want everything all ready when mealtime arrives, wash and scrape the Jerusalem artichokes. As you finish with each one, drop it into acidulated water, made by stirring 1 teaspoon vinegar with a quart of cold water, to prevent it from darkening in the air. Slice or dice. Then cook, covered, in a small amount of boiling salted water

15 to 30 minutes, or until tender. Drain well. Serve with salt, pepper, and butter or margarine, or cream.

The non-starchy Jerusalem artichokes also make memorable salads. One way is to boil them first, then mix 4 cups with 1 finely diced small onion, 1 cup chopped celery, ½ teaspoon salt, a sliced cucumber, and a cup of mayonnaise. Stir together lightly, lifting from the outside in, season, and serve cold.

However, we usually prefer the crisp sweetness of the peeled tubers, which have somewhat the same texture as that of cabbage stalks, just sliced raw and added liberally to tossed salads.

Although not mealy like potatoes, Jerusalem artichokes can be substituted i n many recipes for that common vegetable. For instance, fried slices of the wild edible have a flavor and consistency of their own. When in a hurry I've frequently cooked them in camp this way, sautéing them 8 to 10 minutes with bacon drippings in an already warm frypan and turning them several times during the process. When you have more leisure, they're even better rubbed with oil and baked. Or just add them to a mulligan when it's about half an hour from being done.

When someone in the household is a little under the weather, they may especially enjoy Jerusalem artichokes simmered in milk. Peel about a pound of these healthful tubers and dice them. Drop these small pieces into ¼ cup hot milk, stirring to moisten them well. Cover and cook just below the boiling point for 10 minutes. Then mix in 1 teaspoon salt and 2 tablespoons ground parsley. Sprinkle with paprika and serve while still steaming.

BURDOCK *(Arctium)*

This member of the thistle family marched across Europe with the Roman legions, sailed to the New World with the early settlers, and now thrives throughout much of the United States and southern Canada. A topnotch wild food, it has the added advantages of being familiar and of not being easily mistaken.

BURDOCK

The somewhat unpleasant associations with its name are, at the same time, a disadvantage when it comes to bringing this aggressive but delicious immigrant to the table. Muskrats are sold in some markets as swamp rabbits, while crows find buyers as rooks. But unfortunately in this country burdock is usually just burdock, despite the fact that varieties of it are especially cultivated as prized domestic vegetables in Japan and elsewhere in the Eastern Hemisphere.

Burdock is found almost everywhere it can be close to people and domestic animals—along roads, fences, stone walls, and in yards, vacant lots, and especially around old barns and stables. Its sticky burrs, which attach themselves cosily to man and beast, are familiar nuisances.

The burdock is a coarse biennial weed which, with its branches, rapidly grows to from two to six feet high. The large leaves, growing on long stems, are shaped something like oblong hearts and are rough and purplish with veins. Tiny, tubular, usually magenta flowers appear from June to November, depending on the locality, the second year. These form the prickly stickers, which actually, of course, are the seed pods.

No one need stay hungry very long where the burdock grows, for this versatile edible will furnish a number of different delicacies. It is for the roots, for instance, that they are grown by Japanese throughout the Orient. Only the first-year roots should be used, but these are easy to distinguish as the biennials stemming from them have no flower and burr stalks. We get all we can use from the sides of our horses' corral, where they are easily disengaged. When found in hard ground, however, the deep, slender roots are harder to come by, although they are worth quite a bit of effort.

The tender pith of the root, exposed by peeling, will make an unusually good potherb if sliced like parsnips and simmered for 20 minutes in water to which about ¼ teaspoon baking soda has been added. Then drain, barely cover with fresh boiling water, add a teaspoon of salt, and cook until tender. Serve with butter or margarine spreading on top.

If caught early enough, the young leaves can be boiled in 2 waters and served as greens. If you're hungry, the peeled young leaf stalks are good raw, especially with a little salt. These are also added to green salads and to vegetable soups and are cooked by themselves like asparagus.

It is the rapidly growing flower stalk that furnishes one of the tastier parts of the burdock. When these sprout up the second year, watch them so that you can cut them off just as the blossom heads are starting to appear in late spring or early summer. Every shred of the strong, bitter skin must be peeled off. Then cook the remaining thick, succulent interiors in 2 waters, as you would the roots, and serve hot with butter or margarine.

The pith of the flower stalks has long been used, too, for a candy. One way to make this is by cutting the whitish cores into bite-size sections. Boil these for 15 minutes in water to which ¼ teaspoon baking soda has been added. Drain. Heat what you judge to be an approximately equal weight of sugar in enough hot water to dissolve it, and then add the juice of an orange. Put in the burdock pieces, cook slowly until the syrup is nearly evaporated, drain, and roll in granulated sugar. This never lasts for very long.

The first-year roots, dug either in the fall or early spring, are also used back of beyond as a healing wash for burns, wounds, and skin irritations. One way to make this is by dropping 4 teaspoons of the root into a quart of boiling water and allowing this to stand until cool.

TOOTHWORT *(Dentaria)*

These slender members of the mustard family flourish in moist woods and along streams. The medium-small white or pinkish flowers grow in clusters, their four petals sometimes arranging themselves in the shape of crosses. The smooth stems, six to fourteen inches high, support leaves with toothed margins. The crisp, whitish roots taste like peppery water cress and mild horseradish. Some dozen species grow, often abundantly, across the continent, one western variety whitening the meadows of the Coast Range in the springtime when it blooms.

Cut-leaved toothwort, *Dentaria laciniata,* blossoms from April to June from Quebec and Minnesota south to Louisiana and Florida. The one-half- to three-fourths-inch white or pinkish flowers, nodding together in terminal groups of some six to eight blossoms, rise on stems seven to twelve inches above the ground. These produce slim seedpods about an inch long. The toothed or lobed leaves, a trio of which encircle the stalk below the flowers, are deeply indented into three to five divisions. The name toothwort comes from the little scales or teeth on the long, easily disjointed root. Both this native perennial and its first cousin, just below, are also known as crinkleroot and as pepper-root.

TOOTHWORT
Left: root; *Right:* stem with leaves and flowers.

The two-leaved toothwort, *Dentaria diphylla,* spreads its peppery goodness over much the same range. Again, its four-petalled flowers, which are white and about half an inch long, grow in clusters of six to eight atop a stalk sometimes a foot high. They bloom in May. The main difference is in the leaves which, growing opposite or nearly opposite one another, number two. They are also a bit larger and lighter green than those of the above species, and they have shorter stems. The roots are long and wrinkled.

We often eat the long, crisp roots of these two species, many times just nibbling their refreshing pepperiness while walking or fishing. They also make very palatable additions to meat sandwiches, whose salt helps bring out their flavor. Chopped, they give character to green salads.

Some day when you're having company and want an elegantly nippy cocktail-hour dip, or a sauce to go with a special boiled beef or venison dinner or succulent roast, whip a cup of heavy cream. Then fold in a teaspoon of freshly grated apple and 2 tablespoons freshly grated toothwort root.

We make a camp version of this by melting 2 tablespoons butter or margarine, blending in 2 tablespoons flour, and gradually adding a cup of milk. Cook, preferably in the top of a double boiler, stirring constantly until thick. Then add 2 tablespoons grated toothwort root, ½ teaspoon salt, and a sprinkling of pepper. Cook 5 minutes more, stirring occasionally.

Or when you're too busy with other things, just scrape or grate a couple of tablespoons or so of these pungent, fleshy rootstocks, moisten with a little vinegar, and set on the table in a small covered cup. You haven't lived until you try this sometime with fat roasted or boiled moose.

SPRING BEAUTY (*Claytonia*)

You sometimes come upon thousands of frail little spring beauties, a very close cousin of the succulent miner's lettuce, carpeting sunny stream banks and moist open woods from Alaska to Nova Scotia, south to Florida and Texas. The individually delicate and inconspicuous little flowers, which together make such a spectacular display, range in color from white to pale rose and measure less than an inch across. Their pinkish-veined heads stay open only in sunlight.

These six-to-ten-inch high members of the purslane family, which grow in a number of similar, small-flowered species, are also known as fairy spuds because of their starchy edible roots, which were a favorite Indian food.

SPRING BEAUTY
Left: root; *Right:* stalk with leaves and flowers.

The grasslike to broadly ovate leaves, depending on the species, are also edible, in salads when young and when older, boiled briefly in a small amount of salted water and served as greens. Both ways they are excellent sources of vitamins A and C. The five-petaled flowers, each of which has five tiny stamens, grow in clusters on long weak stems that are often so overweighed that they lie on the ground.

The spring beauty grows from small, potatolike roots that lie several inches below the surface and require a certain amount of digging, although where they are abundant you can amass a respectable number with just a pointed stick. These roundish tubers range in diameter from one-half to two inches, becoming more and more irregular in shape the larger they grow. The best way we have found to clean them is by scouring them with a brush. Because they are boiled with the jackets on, though, this is not too critical a task.

Fifteen minutes of boiling in salted water usually does the job, although if some of the tubers are the larger ones, up to 5 extra minutes may be required. They're done when a fork shoves through without any difficulty. Then just peel and eat, dipping each first into a pool of melted butter or margarine. To me, they taste like particularly choice little potatoes with overtones of chestnut.

EVENING PRIMROSE *(Oenothera)*

The usually bright yellow, but occasionally pink to white, flowers of this fragrant wild edible are familiar to many because of the way they open at dusk, carrying on their activities in the near darkness when their odor and light color attract the night-flying moths, upon whom they depend for fertilization. These showy but short-lived blossoms close their four petals for good the next morning, remain wilted a day or so, and then fall off.

This native food of mule deer, pronghorn, and other North American wildlife has a wide range that extends across the continent from British Columbia to Labrador, south to Texas and Florida. Preferring open, gravelly locations, the evening primrose is common to dry fields and waste places. Its abundant fleshy roots, sweet and nutritious when boiled, caused it to be transplanted to Europe as a food even before the Pilgrims set sail for the New World.

One of the names it has gained through the centuries is king's cure-all, partly because its somewhat astringent qualities have caused it to be used for coughs resulting from colds. A dose is a teaspoonful of the plant, cut small, to a cup of boiling water, drunk cold during the day, a large mouthful at a time. Too, an ointment made from it is said to be beneficial in treating minor skin irritations.

EVENING PRIMROSE
Left: rosette; *Right:* stalk with leaves, flowers, and seed capsules.

This native biennial grows only a round, broad rosette of leaves with toothed or wavy margins the first year. These leaves are from one to six inches long, often lance-shaped, pointed, thickish, and with obvious midribs. The one- to five-foot flower stems, terminated by one- to two-inch loose-spiked blossoms, do not thrust up until the second year. The seed capsules are about an inch in length, oblong, and hairy. After producing them, the plant dies.

The stout, branching roots are good only the first year,

before the evening primrose flowers. Their growth varies with the climate, and so do the times in spring, summer and fall when they are at their mildest and best. A little local experience, therefore, is usually necessary. But it's worthwhile, for peeled and then boiled in 2 changes of salted water until tender, then served hot with butter or margarine, these roots explain why the evening primrose was one of the first wild American edibles taken back to the Old World for cultivation.

We also like to boil ½ dozen good-sized roots in 2 changes of salted water, to remove the pepperiness, until the tines of a fork pierce them easily. Then peel them, slice them lengthwise, and lay them in a baking dish. We then simmer 1 cup brown sugar and 5 tablespoons butter or margarine in ½ cup water until syrupy. This is poured over the roots which go into a moderate oven for 20 minutes, or until candied.

Evening primrose French-fries, too, always seem to be popular with company. Get enough of the roots for 4, for example, peel them, and then slice each lengthwise and cut into pieces as you would for French-fried potatoes. Boil in 2 changes of salted water until a fork will pierce them with a little difficulty. Then drain and cool.

In the meantime, beat 2 eggs and ¼ cup milk. Season 1 cup flour with 1 teaspoon salt and ⅛ teaspoon pepper. Roll the sections in this, dip in the egg mixture, and finally roll in bread crumbs, patting on all of these that will adhere easily. Fry in shallow butter or salad oil until golden brown, drain briefly on absorbent paper, sprinkle with salt, and serve while hot.

CATTAIL *(Typhaceae)*

Who does not know these tall strap-leaved plants with their brown sausagelike heads which, growing in large groups from two to nine feet high, are exclamation points in wet places throughout the temperate and tropical countries of the world?

CATTAIL
Left: leaves, head, and flower spike; *Right:* basal leaves and root.

Although now relatively unused in the United States, where four species thrive, cattails are deliciously edible both raw and cooked from their starchy roots to their cornlike spikes, making them prime emergency foods. Furthermore, the long slender basal leaves, dried and then soaked to make them pliable, provide rush seating for chairs, as well as tough material for mats. As for the fluff of light-colored seeds, which enliven many a winter wind, these will softly fill pillows and provide warm stuffing for comforters.

Cattails are also known in some places as rushes, cossack asparagus, bulrushes, cat-o'-nine-tails, and flags. Sure signs of fresh or brackish water, they are tall, stout-stemmed perennials with thin, stiff, swordlike, green leaves up to six feet long. These have well-developed, round rims at the sheathing bases.

The branched rootstocks creep in crossing tangles a few inches below the usually muddy surface. The flowers grow densely at the tops of the plants in spikes which, first plumply green and finally a shriveling yellow, resemble long bottle brushes and eventually produce millions of tiny, wind-wafted seeds.

These seeds, it so happens, are too small and hairy to be very attractive to birds except to a few like the teal. It is the starchy underground stems that attract such wildlife as muskrat and geese. Too, I've seen moose dipping their huge, ungainly heads where cattails grow.

Another name for this prolific wild edible should be wild corn. Put on boots and have the fun of collecting a few dozen of the greenish yellow flower spikes before they start to become tawny with pollen. Husk off the thin sheaths and, just as you would with the garden vegetable, put while still succulent into rapidly boiling water for a few minutes until tender. Have plenty of butter or margarine by each plate, as these will probably be somewhat roughly dry, and keep each hot stalk liberally swabbed as you feast on it. Eat like corn. You'll end up with a stack of wiry cobs, feeling deliciously satisfied.

Some people object to eating corn on the cob, too, especially when there is company. This problem can be solved by scraping the boiled flower buds from the cobs, mixing 4 cups of these with 2 cups buttered bread crumbs,

2 well-beaten eggs, 1 teaspoon salt, ⅛ teaspoon pepper, and a cup of rich milk. Pour into a casserole, sprinkle generously with paprika, and heat in a moderate oven 15 minutes.

These flower spikes later become profusely golden with thick yellow pollen which, quickly rubbed or shaken into pails or onto a cloth, is also very much edible. A common way to take advantage of this gilded substance, which can be easily cleaned by passing it through a sieve, is by mixing it half and half with regular flour in breadstuffs.

For example, the way to make pleasingly golden cattail pancakes for 4 is by sifting together 1 cup pollen, 1 cup flour, 2 teaspoons baking powder, 2 tablespoons sugar, and ½ teaspoon salt. Beat 2 eggs and stir them into 1 1/3 cups milk, adding 2 tablespoons melted butter or margarine. Then rapidly mix the batter. Pour at once in cakes the size of saucers onto a sparingly greased griddle, short of being smoking hot. Turn each flapjack only once, when the hot cake starts showing small bubbles. The second side takes only about half as long to cook. Serve steaming hot with butter and sugar, with syrup, or with what you will.

It is the tender white insides of about the first 1 or 1½ feet of the peeled young stems that, eaten either raw or cooked, lends this worldwide delicacy its name of cossack asparagus. These highly eatable aquatic herbs can thus be an important survival food in the spring.

Later on, in the fall and winter, quantities of the nutritiously starchy roots can be dug and washed, peeled while still wet, dried, and then ground into a meal which can be sifted to get out any fibers. Too, there is a pithy little tidbit where the new stems sprout out of the rootstocks that can be roasted or boiled like young potatoes. All in all, is it any wonder that the picturesque cattails, now too often neglected except by nesting birds, were once an important Indian food?

Wild Nuts

Some of the most fun I've ever had in the woods, both as a youngster and as an adult, has been when I've gone nutting. If, when leaves are blazing and days are crisp, you've never gathered beechnuts, walnuts, butternuts, or other of the numerous edible wild nuts with which North America is so liberally endowed, then you've never really lived.

The highly nutritious oiliness of nuts causes them to keep best when protected from air, moisture, and warmth. To prolong freshness, store them in a cool, dry place or, ideally, in a refrigerator or freezer. Unshelled nuts last the longest. Nut meats should be kept in well-sealed containers or in moistureproof wrappings. Large pieces stay fresh longer, so it is best not to break, chop, grate, or grind nuts until you are ready to use them.

BLACK WALNUT *(Juglans)*

Six of the world's dozen species of *Juglans* are native to this country. In addition to the common black walnut, whose range extends throughout most of the East and partway into the prairies, there are two species of black walnut in the Southwest and two more in California. Since early colonial days, this leading gunstock wood has been the king of the American cabinet woods. The hulls which enclosed the nuts dyed the homespuns of many of the first settlers.

BLACK WALNUT

The black walnut is a strong and durable tree, often fifty to a hundred feet in height, with a close-grained trunk from two to six feet in diameter. The prominently ridged and furrowed bark is a rich, dark brown. The large compound leaves, one to two feet long, are composed of up to fifteen to twenty-five leaflets, with what would be the topmost one often missing. These somewhat ovally lance-shaped leaflets, from two to four inches long and about half as wide, have pointed tips and sharply toothed edges. Yellowish green on top, they are lighter and generally downy underneath.

During the summer the nuts, covered with a greenish and warty husk, become two to three inches in diameter. Growing alone and in pairs, they ripen about October and soon fall from the widely spreading branches. Underneath this husk is the familiar globular nut, varying up to about two inches in diameter. Sculptured bony shells, as everyone knows, surround the deeply corrugated, furrowed, sweet, four-celled meats.

If you don't buy your walnuts at the store, the hardest part about gathering and using them is getting off the husks with their indelible brownish dye. When we were kids we didn't mind this and, just stamping on the husks and breaking them off with bare fingers, we collected stained hands that defied parental scrubbing for weeks. Today gloves are a more usual precaution. A knife will remove the green hides. Some pioneers also early found out that if they spread the freshly gathered nuts in the sun until they partially dried, the husks were easily shucked off. The wetly stained nuts were then spread out to dry and to lose bitterness until they were ready to be cracked open.

Those of the sweet and somewhat oily kernels that are not eaten on the spot are much in demand for cakes and candies because of their strong and distinctive taste. You no doubt have your own recipes, but here are a few that have become our favorites over the years.

One of the best of these is a nut bannock which even comes out well in a camp oven if you happen to be hunting in the fall where walnuts abound. For a hot loaf large enough for 2 hungry people, thoroughly blend 2 cups flour, ½ cup sugar, 3 teaspoons baking powder, and 1 teaspoon salt. To avoid any unnecessary loss of the leavening carbon dioxide gas from the baking powder, mix in ½ cup broken walnut meats at this time. Stir an egg into a cup of milk. Add this to the dry ingredients, rapidly forming a dough.

Get this without delay into a buttered pan and into a preheated moderate oven. Bake about 45 minutes or until a straw inserted into the loaf comes out clean. If any is left over, it will provide memorable sandwiches for the next day. Although walnuts excel in this baking powder bread, other wild nuts can be substituted.

People who live in the vicinity of both fresh walnuts and dates can combine both to make a most delicious dessert. Cut 2 cups dates into small bits. Add 2 tablespoons butter or margarine and 1 teaspoon baking soda. Pour 2 cups boiling water over everything. Blend well 2 well-beaten eggs, 1 teaspoon vanilla, 2 cups sugar, and 2 cups sifted flour, and stir well into the above mixture. Then fold in 1 cup walnuts, which have been broken into small pieces. Spread out in a greased pan. Bake 40 minutes in a moderately slow oven. Cut into squares and served with whipped cream, this is something to liven the conversation.

If you like walnut fudge, give this recipe at least a try. Melt a ¼-pound stick butter or margarine and 2 ounces bitter chocolate. Sift together 1½ cups sugar, ½ cup cake flour, and ⅛ teaspoon salt, and add it to the above. Stir 3 well-beaten eggs, 1 teaspoon vanilla, and a cup of walnuts, broken into fine pieces, into the mixture. Bake in a moderate oven for 25 minutes. Then cut into squares and make up your own mind.

Eating your first walnut pie is sort of like it used to be to put on your first pair of long pants or high heels. Melt ¼ pound butter or margarine and stir into it 1 cup sugar, 1 cup corn syrup, and 1 teaspoon cinnamon. Beat 3 eggs and add these. Cover 1/3 cup walnuts with a cloth and pound and mash the meats into a pulp. Stir in these, along with 2 tablespoons boiling water. Pour everything into an uncooked 9-inch pie shell and bake in a moderate oven for 50 minutes. This is surprisingly good either hot or cold, although we prefer the former.

BUTTERNUT *(Juglans)*

Confederate soldiers and partisans were referred to as butternuts during the Civil War because of the brown homespun clothes of the military, often dyed with the green nut husks and the inner bark of these familiar trees. Some of the earliest American settlers made the same use of them. As far back as the Revolution, a common laxative was made of the inner bark, a spoonful of finely cut pieces to a cup of boiling water, drunk cold. Indians preceded the colonists in boiling down the sap of this tree, as well as that of the black walnut, to make syrup and sugar, sometimes mixing the former with maple syrup.

BUTTERNUT

The butternut thrives in chillier climates than does the black walnut, ranging higher in the mountains and further north. Otherwise, this tree, also known as white walnut and oilnut, closely resembles its cousin except for being smaller and lighter colored. Its wood is comparatively soft, weak, and light, although still close-grained. The larger trees, furthermore, are nearly always unsound.

Butternuts grow from the Maritime Provinces to Ontario, south to the northern mountainous regions of Georgia and Alabama, and west to Arkansas, Kansas, and the Dakotas. They are medium-sized trees, ordinarily from about thirty to fifty feet high, with a trunk diameter of up to three feet. Some trees, though, tower up to ninety feet or more. The furrowed and broadly ridged bark is grey.

The alternate compound leaves are from fifteen to thirty inches long. Each one is made up of eleven to seventeen lance-shaped, nearly stemless leaflets, two to six inches long and about half as broad, with sharply pointed tips, saw-toothed edges, and unequally rounded bases. Yellowish green on top, these are paler and softly downy underneath. The catkins and the short flower spikes appear in the spring when the leaves are about half grown.

The nuts are oblong rather than round, blunt, about two to two and a half inches long, and a bit more than half as thick. Thin husks, notably sticky and coated with matted rusty hairs, enclose the nuts whose bony shells are roughly ridged, deeply furrowed, and hard. Frequently growing in small clusters of two to five, these ripen in October and soon drop from the branches.

The young nuts, when they have nearly reached their full size, can be picked green and used for pickles which bring out the flavor of meat like few other things and which really attract notice as hors d'oeuvres. If you can still easily shove a large needle through the nuts, it is not too late to pickle them, husks and all, after they have been scalded and the outer fuzz rubbed off.

Put them in a strong brine for a week, changing the water every other day and keeping them tightly covered. Then drain and wipe them. Pierce each nut all the way through several times with a large needle. Then put them in glass jars with a sprinkling of powdered ginger, nutmeg, mace, and cloves between each layer. Bring some good cider vinegar to a boil, immediately fill each jar, and seal. You can start enjoying this unusual delicacy in two weeks.

A noteworthy dessert can be made with butternuts by mixing ½ cup of the broken meats with 1 cup diced dates,

1 cup sugar, 1 teaspoon baking powder, and ⅛ teaspoon salt. Beat 4 egg whites until they are stiff and fold them into the above mixture. Bake in a greased pan in a slow oven for 20 minutes. Serve either hot or cold with whipped cream. This is also good, particularly when hot, with liberal scoops of vanilla ice cream.

Butternut and date pie is something special. Chop a cup apiece of dates and nuts. Roll a dozen ordinary white crackers into small bits, too. Mix with 1 cup sugar and ½ teaspoon baking powder. Then beat 3 egg whites until they are stiff. Sometimes, if the nuts are not as tasty as usual, we also add a teaspoon of almond extract. In either event, fold into the nut mixture and pour into a buttered 9-inch pie pan. Bake ½ hour, or until light brown, in a moderate oven. Cool before cutting. Ice or whipped cream is good with this, too, but it is also delicately tasty alone.

Butternut brownies, eaten by the nibble and washed down with draughts of steaming black tea, are one of the ways I like to top off my noonday lunches when hunting in the late fall. Just blend together 1 cup sugar, 1 teaspoon salt, ½ cup melted butter or margarine, 2 squares bitter chocolate, 1 teaspoon vanilla, and 3 eggs. When this is thoroughly mixed, stir into it 1 cup finely broken butternuts and ½ cup flour. Pour into a shallow greased pan and bake in a moderate oven 20 minutes.

HAZELNUT (*Corylus*)

Three species of hazelnuts are natives of the United States and Canada. Two grow in the East, making these nuts available from Newfoundland all the way across Canada to British Columbia, south to Georgia, Tennessee, and Florida. Another grows in the mountains of California. Incidentally, the filberts sold in stores are cultivated hazelnuts.

The low-spreading thickness of hazelnut bushes provides

useful cover and nesting sites wherever these thickets occur along streams, the edges of woods, pasture slopes, fences, and roadsides. Squirrels and chipmunks feast on the nuts. Grouse pick off the catkins, while deer, moose, and rabbits browse on the plants themselves.

HAZELNUT
Top: beaked hazelnut; *Bottom:* American hazelnut.

The three varieties of this many-branched shrub are much alike, although the nuts differ some. Those of the *Corylus Americana,* growing in open husks, have brown shells that are usually thick and hard. The beaked hazelnut, also of the East, has an exceedingly bristly husk that, instead of likewise flaring at the top, is contracted into a long neck about one and a half inches long. The shell of this nut is more whitish brown and is comparatively thin. The nuts of the California species are larger but similar.

The *Corylus Americana,* to describe one of these species, grows in clumps whose widely spreading branches reach a height of six or seven feet. The young brown growth, which later becomes smooth, is initially furred with pinkish bristles. The alternate short-stemmed leaves, which resemble those of the yellow birch and alder, are egg-shaped or widely oval, with sharp tips and toothed margins.

Slender catkins, which sway in the breezes, make their appearance in early spring before the new leaves burst forth, and grow three or four inches long. The inconspicuous fertile flowers appear in scaly buds near the tips of the branches. The nuts are usually sweet and ripe in August and if not bothered, cling to the shrubs until late in the fall.

If you should want to remove the inner skin from hazelnuts, this can be done without softening them. Just spread them in a pan and heat in a moderate oven 20 to 30 minutes. Do not brown. Let them cool. Then rub off the loosened skins with a towel.

Hazelnut macaroons come alive in your mouth. Chop up 3 cups of hazelnuts or, easier, grind them in an electric blender at high speed until very fine. Beat 5 egg whites with ⅛ teaspoon salt until they stand in peaks. Then gradually beat in 2 cups sifted confectioners' sugar and ½ cup sifted flour. Thoroughly stir in the nuts and 1 teaspoon baking powder. Drop, ½ teaspoon at a time, about 1½ inches apart, on a greased shallow pan or cookie sheet. Bake in a slow oven 15 minutes, or until the edges take on a golden tinge. After they have cooled, keep the 5 dozen or so cookies in a closed container for as long as they last, which isn't likely to be long.

There are many delicately flavored candies you can make with hazelnuts. One of the best of these can be made without cooking. Just mix 1 egg white and 2 cups sifted confectioners' sugar. Add 2 teaspoons butter or margarine and continue to blend until creamy and smooth. Then thoroughly work in 2 cups finely chopped hazelnuts and form into balls. And see who wants to go nutting again tomorrow.

HICKORY (*Carya*)

Hickories are probably our most important native nuts. The
Indians used them in great quantities for food, and the
settlers soon followed suit, even tapping the sweet sap in
the spring for syrup and sugar. Today the nuts are familiar
in the stores of this country.

HICKORY
1 Shagbark; 2 Pignut; 3 Bitternut.

The shellbark hickory, also called the shagbark, is the
leader of the clan, although there are from twenty to twenty-
two other species, depending upon the botanist. All are
edible, although the taste of some is not appealing. There
are the sweet hickories, including the above, in which the
husk splits into 4 parts when the nuts are ripe. There are
the pignuts, often bitter but sometimes delicious, in which
the thin husk splits only above the middle, or, sometimes

late in the season, all the way to the base. There are also the familiar pecans.

The stout twigs and the grey bark which loosens in shaggy narrow strips, attached at the middle, distinguishes the shellbark and the shagbark, actually two different species, from all other trees. The leaves, from seven to fourteen inches long, are composed of usually five but sometimes seven leaflets. Dark yellowish green above, these are lighter and often downy beneath, with fine sharp teeth marking the edges.

Hickories grow slowly, and the shellbark does not produce nuts until about eighty years old. It becomes a large stately tree, reaching a height of up to 180 or more feet and a trunk diameter of one to three feet. Its wood is used for such things as bows, skiis, and ax handles, while hickory-smoked hams and bacon are famous. Wood duck, ring-necked pheasant, bobwhite, and wild turkey compete with man for the nuts. Black bear, raccoon, squirrel, and rabbit eat both nuts and bark, while the white-tailed deer relishes both these and the younger twigs.

The shellbark, which leafs out later than most other trees and sheds its bronze foliage earlier, ranges from Maine and Quebec west to the Great Lakes and Minnesota, and south to northern Florida and eastern Texas. The fruits, varying a great deal in size, are on the average from one to two inches in diameter, nearly round or somewhat oblong, and depressed at the top. The husks, which are about a quarter inch thick, split into four pieces at maturity. The familiar white or tawny nuts are a bit flattened with four ridges, an easily cracked thin shell, and large sweet kernels.

You can have an enjoyable time with just a heap of hickory nuts and a stone or hammer. But the pleasant, slightly aromatic meats also excel in the kitchen.

They can even be cooked with vegetables. Sometimes when you have gathered a bushel or so of nuts, probably from a noble tree in an open field or along the rim of a wood where its branches can stretch far into the sunlight, try cooking some with corn. Whip 2 eggs to a froth. Stir in a teaspoon salt, a tablespoon flour, and a cup of chopped hickory nuts. Add a cup of milk and 2 cups corn, fresh, canned, or frozen. Bake the mixture in a greased dish in a moderate oven until it is firm.

It is in the desserts, though, that the sweet-meat members of the clan are surpassingly good. For instance, it is difficult to outdo the following simple cookies. Just whip the whites of 2 eggs until they are stiff. Beat 2 cups of brown sugar into this. Then add 2 cups nuts that have been broken into small pieces. Drop from a teaspoon, about 1½ inches apart, onto a shallow greased pan or a greased baking sheet. Bake in a slow oven for 35 to 45 minutes or until light brown.

When we are in hickory country, nut balls have become traditional with us for the Christmas season, when neighbors are always dropping in to exchange cheer. You have to crush 2 cups of nuts for this by pounding, rolling, or, most easily, by running through a food grinder. Then blend a cup of butter or margarine with 4 tablespoons sugar and 3 teaspoons vanilla until creamy. Thoroughly mix the nuts with 2 cups sifted flour and stir into the preceding mixture. Shape the dough into little balls slightly larger than marbles. Place on a greased shallow pan or cookie sheet. Bake in a slow oven 45 minutes. Frost by rolling in confectioners' sugar while hot and again when cool. Store those that aren't snatched up immediately in a closed container.

The following pie is delectable with pecans but even better with shellbark hickories. Beat 3 eggs until light. Add 1 cup sugar, 1 cup white corn syrup, a melted ¼-pound stick of butter or margarine, 1½ teaspoons vanilla, and finally, 1 cup chopped nuts. Bake in an uncooked 9-inch pie shell in a moderate oven for about 40 minutes. We don't know of a tastier way to usher in the nutting season.

BEECH *(Fagus)*

The first dawn I ever went deer hunting in New Brunswick, my friend, Sandy Macdonald, saw to it that we were stalking into the wind along the top of a beechnut ridge by the time the late fall sun was wheeling above the horizon. He was right, too. Whitetails, black bear, wood duck, ruffed grouse, and other wildlife vie with man for this important crop which, as Indians and early settlers well knew, is one

BEECH

Left: winter twig; *Top center:* branch with mature leaves and burrs; *Bottom center:* nut; *Right:* branch with early leaves and sterile and fertile blossoms.

of the most flavorful products of our northern forests.

The now largely cleared beechnut forests of the Middle West were once the gathering places of the also departed passenger pigeons, which subsisted to a large extent on the nuts. Our single native species of this tree grows from the Maritime Provinces to Ontario and Wisconsin, southward to eastern Texas and northern Florida. The large handsome trees, with their bright emerald foliage that oxidizes to a magnificent copper or gold in the autumn, are also planted for shade and landscaping. Unfortunately, however, the nuts are by far most numerous only where the trees grow in the northern states and in Canada.

The beech is readily identified throughout the year by its smooth, attractively dappled, bluish-grey bark, which in frequented places, especially when the trunks are two to three feet through, often invites the carving of initials. The trees, up to 100 feet tall, have greatly forked branches that end in numerous delicate grey twigs.

The oblong or oval alternate leaves, almost twice as long as they are wide, have pointed tips and rounded or wedge-shaped bases. Straight-ribbed and coarsely toothed, they are thin and somewhat papery, smoothly emerald green above and yellower and paler beneath. Their short stems, one-fourth to one-half inch long, have a somewhat hairy silkiness.

Both sterile and wind-pollinated fertile blossoms grow on the same tree. The former appear in balls that dangle on long stems. The latter grow in pairs where the upper leaves meet the twigs, developing into small, four-part burrs, softly bristling with recurved hairs. Easily opened by the thumb-nail when they mature in October, these contain two tri-angular, somewhat concave, brown nuts that are nutritious and sweet.

Mostly, I've gathered beechnuts in New England and the Maritimes after heavy frosts have dropped them to the ground. They are so small and delicious that we've always eaten a large proportion of them raw, but they are good cooked, too. Although I've never tried it, a friend of mine at Seven Mile Lake in New Brunswick roasts and grinds them for a beverage which he says tastes like coffee. The young leaves may be cooked as a green in the spring. The inner bark, dried and pulverized for bread flour in times of need in Europe, is an emergency food to remember.

Beechnut and date cakes taste just as good as they smell. Stir 1 teaspoon baking soda into 2 cups boiling water and pour over 1 cup chopped dates. Let stand 10 minutes. Then mix 3 tablespoons butter or margarine, 2 eggs, 3 cups flour, and 2 cups sugar. Stir well into the date mixture. Fold a cup of broken nut meats into all this. Spread in a greased pan and bake 40 minutes in a moderate oven. Cut into squares. Serve those you don't eat on the spot with whipped cream.

When we're East, we try to have beechnut pie several times each autumn. One cup of beechnuts will do for this, too. Thoroughly whip 3 eggs. Then slowly beat into them a ¼-pound stick of melted butter or margarine, 1 cup white corn syrup, and ¾ cup sugar. Turn into an uncooked 9-inch pie shell and bake in a slow oven for 35 minutes. Remove the pie long enough to cover it quickly with nuts. Then return it to the oven, turn up the heat to moderate, and bake another 15 minutes. The only trouble with this is that it encourages you to rush through the rest of your meal to get at it.

Wild Beverages

Indians depended largely on edible wild plants for their beverages. When the first settlers arrived, and for centuries afterward as they were pushing their way westward, they followed suit. If these wild drinks had not been rich in Vitamin C, a vitamin which the body cannot store and which is necessary for the prevention and cure of scurvy, many pioneers could not have lived to open our frontiers.

At the time of the American Revolution, even in the communities where stores were well stocked, many chose wild drinks rather than continue to use oriental tea, tinged with an English tax. When the Civil War tore the country apart, many northerners and southerners alike had to turn again to the wilds for their teas and coffees.

The earlier described wild fruit juices are all refreshing. So are the previously mentioned wild teas brewed from roses, strawberry leaves, raspberry leaves, blackberry leaves, kinnikinic, wintergreen, fireweed, plantain, clover, shepherd's purse, and water cress. This holds true, too, for the coffee substitutes made from dandelion roots, chicory roots, and beechnuts. Then there are the following excellent wild beverage sources.

SPEARMINT *(Mentha)*

Spearmint, the source of the familiar chewing gum flavor and a boon to cookery from ancient times to the present, can be found along damp roadsides and waterways and in wet places from Nova Scotia to British Columbia, south to the Gulf of Mexico and California. The long, creeping roots of this aromatic perennial spread it rapidly.

SPEARMINT

About twelve to twenty inches high, the spearmint is branched and has oblong or lance-shaped green leaves growing opposite each other. These are stemless or nearly so, 1 to 2 inches long, toothed, pointed, veiny, and wrinkled. Tiny, light purple or almost white flowers encircle slender, leafless spikes in the summertime.

Wild mints, as a whole, are quickly identified by their square stems, opposite leaves, and familiar aroma. This characteristic fragrance may be lacking if just a few plants grow together, but you've only to crush a single leaf between your fingers to catch it.

You can find wild mint almost anywhere. I'll never forget the time I took a southern friend of mine hunting in a remote section of British Columbia, two days north of the nearest railhead. Charlie was pretty tired and thirsty by the time we had set up camp by a mountain lake in the late afternoon, especially as the last part of the trip had been made on horseback.

However, he let himself be persuaded that now was a good time of day to see if anything was stirring. We'd no sooner cut some grizzly tracks beside the water, though, than we ran into what must have been an acre of wild mint. The unmistakable odor ended the hunt right there, bear tracks or no, and in less than a half hour Charlie had us back by our tent sipping improvised mint juleps.

Wild mint sprigs also give a welcome piquancy to instant iced tea made with one of the dehydrated powders. Or if you want something really special for a hot day, make 3 cups of double-strength tea. When this is ready, pour it over a tablespoon of mint jelly and stir until the latter is dissolved. Chill. Fill glasses half full of tea. Add crushed ice, and then fill to the rims with cold ginger ale. Garnish with mint sprigs.

Wild mint vinegar has an agreeableness all its own. You can make it by filling a jar loosely with fresh green sprigs of wild mint. Cover with ordinary cider vinegar. Then close the jar and place on a sunny windowsill for 3 weeks. At the end of this time, strain and rebottle.

For a mint sauce to serve hot over lamb or well-done roast venison still sizzling from the oven, mix a tablespoon of sugar with ½ cup mild cider vinegar, diluted with water, if too strong. Pour this over ½ cup torn mint leaves and let stand ½ hour over low heat. Or if you're going to use it cold, just bring the sugar and vinegar to a bubble, add the leaves, let boil up briefly, and then set aside to cool.

Mint jelly is something we particularly like when we're living in the woods and eating lots of meat. Wash and quarter 4 quarts unpeeled and uncored apples, put in a kettle, barely cover with cold water, and simmer until soft. Then mash, drain through 4 thicknesses of dampened cheesecloth, and measure. Add an equal volume of sugar. Bring again to a bubble, add ½ cup fresh mint leaves and 2 tablespoons lemon juice, and boil until a spoonful runs off the side of the spoon in a sheet. Strain into hot glasses and cover immediately with melted paraffin.

A quicker method is boiling 3 cups apple cider with ½ cup fresh mint leaves for 15 minutes and then straining through a sieve. Stir a package of pectin into the juice and, continuing to stir, bring to a boil. Now gradually add 4 cups sugar and continue stirring until a full rolling boil is reached. Boil 2 minutes. Then remove from the heat, stir in 4 tablespoons cider vinegar, skim, and pour as usual into hot sterilized glasses, sealing these at once with hot paraffin. To avoid losing track of fruit if you put up very much, label and date all batches.

OSWEGO TEA (*Monarda*)

Early settlers found this family of native perennials an excellent substitute for tea, especially in the backwoods where supplies were limited and in populated regions during the American Revolution. We have also used the minty leaves as a flavor in cooking. The fragrant plants with their showy flowers are also known as beebalm, wild bergamot, and horsemint. They grow from Quebec to British Columbia, south to Tennessee and Georgia.

The Oswego teas are rather coarse plants two to three feet tall, with beautiful large flowers that vary in color from scarlet to lavender. In fact, their beauty enhances the occasional garden, and some species brought from Europe have gone wild. Their square stems, opposite leaves, and the aroma of their crushed foliage identify them as members of the mint family. The dark green, aromatic leaves, two to six inches long, are sharp-toothed. The very pretty blossoms, almost

OSWEGO TEA

two inches broad, adorn these mints from July to September.

To brew Oswego tea, use ½ to 1 teaspoon of the dried leaves, according to taste, for each cup of boiling water. If you are using fresh leaves, double the quantity. Let steep 5 minutes. We prefer this plain, but some of our friends like to add sugar, milk, or both.

Incidentally, the best way to dry the wild teas is at room, never oven, temperature. Just hang a bagful near the ceiling for a few weeks. Then store in closed jars and keep in a cool dark place, so as to retain as much of the volatile aroma as possible.

WILD COFFEE *(Triosteum)*

Wild coffee has also collected the names of feverwort, tinker's weed, and horse gentian. The three species of this coarse perennial grow in open woods and along roadsides, slopes, walls, and fences from New England to Nebraska, south to Alabama and Missouri. They are more of the wild plants used as beverages during colonial days.

WILD COFFEE

Wild coffee has rather hairy stems up to three or four feet high. The opposite leaves, which narrow abruptly at their bases, often encircle the stem. The reddish or orange berries, which are egg-shaped to nearly spherical and about half an inch long, grow in small clusters in the joints between leaves and stems. Each contains a trio of large seeds.

Dried, roasted, and ground, these berries may be used instead of coffee. Put into fresh cold water, using 2 level teaspoons for every cup of water. Amounts can be varied, of course, for a stronger or weaker brew. Set this on the heat. Watch it carefully. As soon as it boils up once, lift it off to take on body for 5 minutes. Then settle the grounds, if you want, with a couple of tablespoons of cold water and start pouring.

KENTUCKY COFFEE TREE (*Gymnocladus*)

Roasted and ground, the seeds of the Kentucky coffee tree were used by early settlers in the New World as a substitute for coffee. Some of the Indians roasted them and ate them like nuts. The trees, often planted today for shade and for

KENTUCKY COFFEE TREE

landscaping, range from New York to southern Minnesota, south to Tennessee and Oklahoma.

Usually a medium-sized tree, reaching a height of forty to ninety feet and a trunk diameter of from one to three feet, the Kentucky coffee tree ordinarily branches a few feet above the ground into three or four limbs which climb almost vertically to form a narrow crown.

The dark green leaves, which remain on for only about half of the year, are sometimes almost three feet long and two feet wide. They are composed of up to forty or more short-stemmed leaflets. Long clusters of greenish-white flowers appear in June. These develop into reddish-brown pods from four to ten inches long and from one to two inches wide. Each contains six to nine large, oval, flat, hard brownish seeds encased in a dark sweetish pulp.

You can roast these seeds slowly in the oven, grind them, and brew them like coffee. They have none of the caffeine of regular coffee, and the resulting beverage agrees with some people better.

SWEET FERN *(Myrica) (Comptonia)*

The fragrant leaves of the sweet fern were used as a tea as far back as the American Revolution. This plant is actually a shrub, partial to open fields and upland slopes where trees are sparse or absent, often forming solid stands in such habitats. It is also found to a lesser degree in open woods. Deer browse on it, and game birds and rabbits sometimes seek it out for food. It grows from the Maritimes to Saskatchewan and Minnesota, south to North Carolina, Georgia, Tennessee, and Indiana.

This sweet-scented shrub, growing from one to three feet tall, has fernlike leaves that give it its name. These are deeply divided into many roundish sections, the edges of which are usually sparingly toothed. The male flowers, about an inch in length, grow in clusters at the ends of the slim branches in catkins approximately one inch long. The female flowers grow in egg-shaped catkins. The resulting bristly round burrs envelop hard, glossy, brown little nuts. If you don't mind getting your thumbnail yellow, these are easily exposed and enjoyed, especially during June and early July while they are still tender.

SWEET FERN
Left: branch with leaves; *right*: burr.

The dried aromatic leaves of the sweet fern, a teaspoon to each cup of boiling water, make a very pleasant tea. When you use them fresh, just double the amount.

We've also brewed this in the sun by filling a quart bottle with cold water, adding 8 teaspoons of the fresh leaves, covering the glass with aluminum foil, and setting in the sun. The length of time required depends, of course, upon how hot the sunlight is. The several times I tried this in New

Hampshire, about 3 midday hours were needed before the brew became sufficiently dark. Made this way, wild teas have no bitterness of acrid oils extracted by other methods. You can then strain it, dilute it to individual taste, and serve it with ice.

SASSAFRAS *(Sassafras)*

There is just one species of the familiarly fragrant sassafras that is native to North America. Ours is a small or medium-sized tree, growing from New England to Ontario, Iowa, and Kansas, south to the Gulf of Mexico.

SASSAFRAS
Left: flowers; *Right:* twig with leaves and fruit.

This member of the laurel family, which also includes several trees whose bark is powdered to provide cinnamon, is found along fences and roads, in abandoned fields, in dry woods, and in other open and semi-open places. Thickets often spring up from the roots. Famous for its supposed medicinal qualities soon after Columbus voyaged here, sassafras is now employed commercially mainly as a flavor. Privately, though, it is still widely used for everything from jelly to gumbo.

The very limber twigs and young shoots of the easily recognized sassafras are bright green and mucilaginous. The leaves, aromatic when crushed, grow in three shapes as shown in the drawing, all varieties sometimes stemming from the same twig. Also mucilaginous, they oxidize in the autumn to beautiful reds and oranges. Greenish-gold flowers, which have a spicy odor, appear with the leaves in the spring, the sexes on separate trees. Birds flock to the dark bluish fruits, nearly half an inch long, when they ripen on their thick red stems in the fall.

Sassafras tea, famous for centuries on this continent, where many people still drink it as a spring tonic, can be made by putting a palmful of preferably young roots into a pot with cold water and boiling them until the rich red color that you've learned by experience you like best is reached. Second and third extractions can be made from the same roots.

For drying and storing some of the makings, use just the bark of the young roots. Older roots can be employed, too, but it is best to scrape off the usual hard, rough covering first.

We like this tea sweetened. Only moderate amounts should be used, in any event, as an overdose of the oil may have a narcotic effect. But you can drink too much ordinary tea, too.

With the help of lemon juice, commercial pectin, and sugar, spicy jellies are made of strong sassafras teas. The dainty green winter buds are delicious, and later the young leaves will add flavor to a salad.

In the South, soups are flavored and thickened by the dried leaves, the veins and hard portions of which are first discarded. If you like the wholesome thickness and smoothness of gumbos, why not try this for yourself? The easiest way to go about it is by drying the young tender stems and leaves, grinding them to a fine powder, sifting this through a sieve to remove the hard parts, and pouring the remainder into a large saltshaker for everyone at the table to use according to his own pleasure.

SPICEBUSH *(Benzoin)*

The young leaves, twigs, and bark of the spicebush provide
another of the wild teas much used on this continent, especially in the early days when remoteness and wars made
oriental blends scarce commodities. They provide a pleasant drink, especially if you happen to prefer your tea with
milk and sugar.

SPICEBUSH
Left: branch with leaves; *Right*: branch with flowers.

Two species of the aromatic-leaved spicebush are native
to North America, both being common undergrowths in
swampy woods, along stream banks, and on moist bottomlands. The northern species is found from Maine to Michigan,
south to Georgia and Kansas. A similar species, but with
downy branches and leaves, grows in the southern states.
Like other familiar wild edibles, these cousins of the sassafras have a variety of local names including spicewood, spice,
snapwood, wild allspice, and Benjamin bush. Sometime in
the past, feverbush and feverwood were added because of
the use of this tea in pioneer days to reduce fever.

The spicebush is a shrub, up to some fifteen feet tall, with smooth bark and slim, brittle twigs. Its dark emerald leaves—short-stemmed, thin, smoothly edged, oval or oblong, from three to five inches long, prominently veined, and pointed—change to gold in the fall. The dense clusters of yellow flowers, whose spicy fragrance precedes the leaves in the spring, grow like those of the sassafras with one sex to a shrub. Ring-necked pheasant and bobwhite quail relish the spiciness and oiliness of the oval reddish fruits, each of which contains a single large seed of similar shape.

A handful of young twigs, leaves, or bark simmered for 15 minutes in 4 cups of water makes an aromatic tea. Some people use the berries for this purpose, too. Dried and powdered, these also provide a substitute for allspice. If you become thirsty and dry while outdoors, chewing the pleasantly flavored young bark is an enjoyable way to start the saliva flowing again.

SUMAC *(Rhus)*

Sumac "lemonade" is just the thing to take the edges off a hard afternoon. Pick over a generous handful of the red berries, drop them into a pan and mash them slightly, cover with boiling water, and allow to steep away from any heat until this is well colored. Then strain through 2 thicknesses of cloth to remove the fine hairs. Sweeten to taste, and serve either hot or cold.

Some Indian tribes liked this acid drink so much that they dried the small one-seeded berries and stored them for winter use. Many settlers followed suit.

The rapidly growing staghorn sumac, also called the lemonade tree and the vinegar tree, is one of the largest species of the cashew family, commonly reaching ten to twenty feet in height. It is easily recognized at any season because of the close resemblance of its stout and velvety twigs to deer antlers while these are still in velvet. It ranges from the Maritime Provinces to Ontario, south to Georgia and Missouri.

The bark of these shrubs or small trees, which often form thickets, is smooth. The satiny and often streaked wood, sometimes used commercially for such small objects as napkin rings, is green to orange in color. The fernlike leaves, about fourteen to twenty-four inches long, are composed of eleven to thirty-one pointed leaflets from two to five inches in length. Dark green and smooth above, pale and sometimes softly hairy beneath, these flame into brilliant red in the fall.

STAGHORN SUMAC
Left: winter twig; *Right*: branch with leaves and fruit cluster.

The tiny, tawnily green flowers grow in loosely stemmed clusters, one sex to a shrub or tree. The male clusters are occasionally ten to twelve inches long. The female blossoms are smaller and extremely dense, producing compact bunches of berries. These are erect and so startlingly red that sometimes I've come upon a lone cluster suddenly in the woods and thought it was a scarlet tanager perched on a branch.

The hard red fruits are thickly covered with bright red hairs. These hairs are tart with malic acid, the same flavorsome ingredient found in grapes. Since this is readily soluble in water, the berries should be gathered for beverage purposes before any heavy storms, if possible.

Incidentally, the berries of the poisonous sumacs are white. However, there are other sumacs in the United States and Canada with similar red berries that provide a refreshing substitute for pink lemonade. All these red-fruited species are harmless.

One of them is the smooth or scarlet sumac, *Rhus glabra,* which grows from the Maritimes to Minnesota, south to Florida and Louisiana. This closely resembles the staghorn sumac, except that it is entirely smooth, with a pale bluish or whitish bloom coating the plump twigs.

Another is the dwarf, shining, or mountain sumac, *Rhus copallina,* which grows from New England and Ontario to Florida and Texas. Although similar to the aforementioned species, it can be distinguished from all other sumacs because of peculiar winglike projections along the leaf stems between the leaflets.

Indians made a poultice of the bruised leaves and fruit of the red-berried sumacs and applied it to irritated skin. An astringent gargle, made by boiling the crushed berries in a small amount of water, is still used for sore throats.

BIRCH *(Betula)*

The nutritious bark of the black birch is said to have probably saved the lives of scores of Confederate soldiers during Garnett's retreat over the mountains to Monterey, Virginia. For years afterward, the way the soldiers went could be followed by the peeled birch trees.

The black birch may be identified at all times of the year by its tight, reddish-brown, cherrylike bark, which has the aroma and flavor of wintergreen. Smooth in young trees, this darkens and separates into large, irregular sections as these birches age. The darkly dull green leaves, paler and yellower beneath, are two to four inches long, oval to oblong, short-stemmed, silky when young, smooth when mature, with double-toothed edges. They give off an odor of wintergreen when bruised. The trees have both erect and hanging catkins, on twigs that also taste and smell like wintergreen.

BLACK BIRCH

In fact, when the commercial oil of wintergreen is not made synthetically, it is distilled from the twigs and bark of the black birch. This oil is exactly the same as that from the little wintergreen plant, described earlier.

Black birches enhance the countryside from New England to Ontario, south to Ohio and Delaware, and along the Appalachian Mountains to Georgia and Alabama.

A piquant tea, brisk with wintergreen, is made from the

young twigs, young leaves, the thick inner bark, and the bark from the larger roots. This latter reddish bark, easily stripped off in the spring and early summer, can be dried at room temperatures and stored in sealed jars in a cool place for later use. A teaspoon to a cup of boiling water, set off the heat and allowed to steep for 5 minutes, makes a tea that is delicately spicy. Milk and sugar make it even better. As a matter of fact, any of the birches make good tea.

You can make syrup and sugar from the sap, too, as from the sap of all birches. I'll never forget my first introduction to this. It was our first spring in the paper birch country of the Far North, and Vena and I were bemoaning the fact that there were no maples from which to tap sap for our sourdough pancakes.

"Birch syrup you can get here in copious amounts," Dudley Shaw, a trapper and our nearest neighbor, informed Vena. "Heavenly concoction. It'll cheer Brad up vastly."

"Oh, will you show me how?"

"I'll stow a gimlet in my pack when I prowl up this way the first of the week to retrieve a couple of traps that got frozen in," Dudley agreed. "Noble lap, birch syrup is. Glorious on flippers."

Dudley told us to get some containers. Lard pails would do, he said, or we could attach some wire bails through nail holes in the tops of several tomato cans. He beamed approval when he arrived early Tuesday morning. The improvised sap buckets, suspended on nails driven above the small holes Dudley bored with his gimlet, caught a dripping flow of watery fluid.

"You'd better ramble out this way regularly to see these don't overflow," Dudley cautioned. "Keep the emptied sap simmering cheerfully on the back of the stove. Tons of steam have to come off."

"Will it hurt the trees any?" Vena asked anxiously.

"No, no," Dudley said reassuringly. "The plunder will

begin to bog down when the day cools, anyway. Then we'll whittle out pegs and drive them in to close the blinking holes. Everything will be noble."

Everything was, especially the birch syrup. It wasn't as thick as it might have been, even after all that boiling. There was a distressingly small amount of it, too. But what remained from the day's work was sweet, spicy, and poignantly delicious. What we drank beforehand, too, was refreshing, sweet, and provocatively spicy.

All the birches furnish prime emergency food. Two general varieties of the trees grow across the continent, the black birch and those similar to it, and the familiar white birches whose cheerful foliage and softly gleaming bark lighten the northern forests. Layer after layer of this latter bark can be easily stripped off in great sheets, although because of the resulting disfigurement this shouldn't be done except in an emergency, and used to start a campfire in any sort of weather.

The inner bark, dried and then ground into flour, has often been used by Indians and frontiersmen for bread. It is also cut into strips and boiled like noodles in stews. But you don't need to go even to that much trouble. Just eat it raw.

LABRADOR TEA *(Ledum)*

Labrador tea, also known as Hudson's Bay tea across much of the North where the Hudson's Bay Company maintains its red-roofed white trading posts, is a pretty evergreen shrub whose robustly aromatic leaves still make one of the most famous teas of the north country. It is found growing densely in woods, muskegs, bogs, swamps, damp mountain meadows, and across the tundras of Alaska and Canada south to New England, Pennsylvania, New Jersey, and the Great Lake states, where it is seen mainly in mountain bogs and swamps. Its leaves were among those gathered for tea during the American Revolution.

Labrador tea is easy to distinguish, being a resinous ever-green shrub, ranging from one to four feet high, which is so attractive that two centuries ago the English brought it back to embellish their gardens. The telltale features are the alternate, dryly leathery, fragrant leaves whose smooth edges roll inward toward densely woolly undersides. These darken from greyish to reddish brown, as the otherwise green leaves age. These very distinctive, thickish leaves are usually less than two inches in length, although I have seen them as long as four inches.

LABRADOR TEA

Left: branch with leaves and buds; *Center:* branches with leaves and flowers; *Right:* branches with seed pods.

This member of the heath family, which is eaten by moose and deer, blooms with tiny white flowers that, growing on slender individual stems, form showy, umbrellalike clusters at the tops of woolly stalks. These later provide slim seed-pods.

Available in winter as well as during the warm months, the spicy leaves of Labrador tea make a palatable and refreshing tea. Although I seldom bother to measure exactly, about 1 tablespoon per cup, heaping or otherwise, depending on your particular palate, will make a pleasant brew. Drop them into bubbling water and immediately set this away from the heat to steep for 5 minutes.

Old sourdoughs have warned me that drunk in too large quantities this tea may have a cathartic effect. But, using it sparingly over the years, I have never experienced any ill effects. As a matter of fact, I often find it both refreshing and thirst-quenching to chew on a few leaves while hunting or getting in wood.

NEW JERSEY TEA *(Ceanothus)*

Possibly the most noteworthy of the native American beverage plants is the widely growing New Jersey tea, also known as redroot because of the color of its roots, which make a fine dye. The leaves of this common shrub, both green and dried, were regularly brewed in the thirteen colonies when, around the time of the Boston Tea Party and later during the Revolution, oriental blends were both in disfavor and scarce. More than one soldier under General Washington's command kept up his spirits with such pleasantly flavored infusions which, even if they lacked the caffeine of the more familiar tea, were at least hot and bracing.

Despite its name, New Jersey tea is found in dry open woods and on sandy or gravelly banks from New England to Manitoba, south to the Gulf of Mexico from Florida to Texas. It is a low shrub with erect branches, commonly growing in small bunches from the same group of roots, that reach from about one to three feet in height and then die back from the tips downward.

This member of the buckthorn family, also sometimes called wild snowball, has a large root with a thickish red or brownish bark which is sometimes used, a teaspoon to a cup of boiling water, to make a gargle.

NEW JERSEY TEA
Left: bud and leaf scar; *Center*: stalk with leaves and flowers; *Right*: fruit.

The alternate leaves, growing on short stems, are oval and pointed, with edges reminiscent of a blunt fine-toothed saw. Up to about three inches long and somewhat less than half as wide, they have dark green tops and pale undersides that are marked by three very definite ribs. The minute white flowers, which attract quantities of insects when they appear from June to August, grow in very noticeable, long-stemmed clusters on the tops of the branches. The fruit is a dry, three-lobed capsule.

Although the freshly picked leaves make a flavorful enough

beverage, this is considerably improved if they are dried first, especially if sugar and cream are added. We gather several small paper bagfuls of the leaves while the plant is still in blossom and hang them near the ceiling for several months. Measure and use like oriental tea.

HEMLOCK *(Tsuga)*

Hemlock tea is famous in northern New England and Canada. Drunk hot and black, its taste is reminiscent of the way a Christmas tree smells. More important for trappers, prospectors, and other outdoorsmen, this tea contains the vital Vitamin C.

HEMLOCK

Of the seven to nine species of hemlocks recognized in the world, four are native to North America. These tall, straight evergreens are typical of cool, damp slopes, ravines, and swamps, generally in northern regions and in the higher mountains. They also spring up after tree-cutting operations, their low dense foliage affording fine winter cover for grouse, turkey, deer, and other wildlife.

The needles grow in spirals, although they often seem to be attached in two ranks. The hanging cones have thin segments which hide a pair of tiny winged seeds that are important food for birds and red squirrels. Hemlocks in New England and the Maritimes are often killed by porcupines eating the bark.

Incidentally, these conifers are no relation whatsoever to the poison hemlock from which Socrates and other ancients brewed their deadly draughts. Those entirely different plants are members of the parsley family.

It doesn't really make too much difference if you mistake one of the other conifers for hemlock. All these members of the pine family provide aromatic and beneficial tea. The bright green young tips, when they appear in the springtime, are best. These are tender and starchy at this time and can also be enjoyed raw. Older green needles will do, too. I just put a handful in a receptacle, cover them with boiling water, and let them steep until the tea tastes strong enough. If you prefer this black as I do, there's no need of any straining. Just narrow your lips on the rim and quaff it down.

The hemlocks and other members of the great pine family, which includes the numerous pines themselves, the spruces, firs, balsams, and all the others, have another feature which, if one is ever lost or stranded, can mean the difference between life and death. The inner bark can be cut off and eaten, either raw or boiled, to provide strength and nourishment.